"I Sure Wish This Dam Thing Was Over"

The WW II Letters and Experiences of Private Carl E. Meyers

Charles R. Meyers and Christopher C. Meyers

Hamilton Books

An Imprint of
Rowman & Littlefield
Lanham • Boulder • New York • Toronto • Plymouth, UK

Copyright © 2016 by Hamilton Books
4501 Forbes Boulevard, Suite 200, Lanham, Maryland 20706
Hamilton Books Acquisitions Department (301) 459-3366

Unit A, Whitacre Mews, 26-34 Stannary Street,
London SE11 4AB, United Kingdom

All rights reserved
Printed in the United States of America
British Library Cataloguing in Publication Information Available

Library of Congress Control Number: 2015949680
ISBN: 978-0-7618-6668-8 (pbk : alk. paper)—ISBN: 978-0-7618-6669-5 (electronic)

∞™ The paper used in this publication meets the minimum requirements of American National Standard for Information Sciences Permanence of Paper for Printed Library Materials, ANSI/NISO Z39.48-1992.

Dedicated to the memory of Florence Meyers (later Florence Watt),
Wife of Carl E. Meyers
Mother of Charles R. Meyers
Grandmother of Christopher C. Meyers

Contents

Acknowledgments		vii
Introduction		1
1	Conscription and Basic Training	5
2	The Letters from Basic Training	21
3	In the European Theater of Operations	79
4	The Letters from Europe	95
5	Afterword	103
Bibliography		107
Index		109

Acknowledgments

One of the pleasant tasks of writing this book is thanking those who helped and assisted in completing the project, and we have many debts to recognize. Archivists and librarians at numerous repositories across the country are among the most important resources to historians conducting research. We particularly wish to thank the staffs of the National Archives, the National Personnel Records Center in St. Louis, and the Department of the Army's U.S. Total Army Personnel Command in Alexandria, VA for their assistance with our many requests for documents. Likewise, the staffs at the Lima Public Library in Lima, OH and Wright State University in Dayton, OH were generous with their time and microfilm collections of Ohio newspapers. The U.S. Army Center of Military History permitted us to use the maps that appear in the book.

Our family was a constant source of encouragement and moral support: Jill Meyers, Shirley Woods, Caren Meyers Rom, Julie Meyers, Tracy Carter, and Jacob Meyers. Friends also provided encouragement, particularly Bob Spillman, Lee Pyles, Paul Riggs, Jim Martinello, and Shelley Stiver Brannon.

Our greatest debt of gratitude, however, goes to Florence Meyers, without whom this project could not been completed and to whom this book is dedicated. Florence was married to Carl Meyers and, unbeknownst to anyone else, kept and preserved the letters Private Meyers wrote to her while he was in the Army.

Introduction

In accepting his party's nomination for President at the 1936 Democratic Nominating Convention on June 27, 1936, President Franklin D. Roosevelt said, "This generation of Americans has a rendezvous with destiny."[1] Indeed this generation, which had already experienced the mass consumption of the 1920s and the Great Depression of the 1930s, still had one more "destiny" to face. Although the guns of war had not yet begun to fire when Roosevelt made his statement, this generation of Americans would help the Allies win the Second World War. One of those Americans who took part in this rendezvous was Ohioan Carl Edgar Meyers.

This book chronicles the letters and experiences of Carl Meyers while he served in the U.S. Army during World War II. He wrote 76 letters home to his wife Florence while he was in basic training and another 14 when he was in Europe; the letters date from March to November 1944. During his basic training (March-July) Meyers was a frequent correspondent, never letting more than three days lapse between letters. While in Europe (September-November) he wrote less frequently, usually every four or five days. The existence of the letters remained largely unknown for almost 45 years. After Meyers was killed in the war, his wife Florence put them away in a drawer and there they remained. When Florence passed away in 1988, her children Charles and Shirley discovered the letters along with their father's Purple Heart commendation. This volume outlines how Carl Meyers experienced World War II.

The letters here are separated between those Meyers wrote while in basic training and those he wrote from Europe; they are in separate chapters, and are annotated to introduce people and explain events that may not be common knowledge. The wording of the letters was not changed and nothing in them was corrected; we did not insert [sic] after each misspelling, as that would interrupt the flow of the letters. We felt no need to "sanitize" the letters by correcting the grammar, spelling, and punctuation; this gives a more accurate historical depiction of an average American soldier (and average American) during the mid-1940s. There is a narrative chapter for each category of letters (basic training and Europe) that places the letters and Carl Meyers into the appropriate historical context. Chapter 1 is the narrative for the letters from basic training, while chapter 3 is the narrative for the European letters; chapters 2 and 4 are the annotated letters. An afterword describes his burial in France and the return of his remains to Ohio.

The significance of the letters and accompanying narrative is that Carl Meyers is an example of how the average drafted soldier experienced World War II. From registering for the draft in 1940, to being drafted in 1944, to seeing action on the front lines, Meyers represented how typical American GIs fought the war. Meyers's war experiences were not extraordinary—he fought for his country and died for his country like thousands of other men. Perhaps this volume can provide insight into what the war was like for combat infantrymen.

NOTE

1. *The Public Papers and Addresses of Franklin D. Roosevelt*, Volume 5 (New York: Random House, 1938), 235.

Portrait of Carl Meyers taken while he was in basic training at Camp Fannin, 1944. Photo in possession of the authors.

Chapter One

Conscription and Basic Training

Born on August 11, 1910, Carl Meyers spent the bulk of his 34 years in Harrod and Lima, in Allen County, Ohio and Waynesfield, in Auglaize County, Ohio. He was born in the village of Harrod, which was in the eastern part of Allen County and is currently included in the Lima Metropolitan Statistical Area. Harrod boasted a population of 474 in 1910, and Carl Meyers grew up there along with his eight siblings, five brothers (Ortez, Solomon, Howard, Walter, and Robert) and three sisters (Etta, Glenna, and Sara). He never lacked for playmates. Meyers attended Harrod High School, part of a nineteen-member freshman class. Following high school, he lived in Harrod and worked at a variety of places, including the local furniture store. In his mid-20s he met Florence Seaman of Waynesfield; they married on August 31, 1936, and the two moved to her hometown, in neighboring Auglaize County. The move was relatively short, as Auglaize County is the next county south of Allen (Auglaize County, in fact, was formed out of the southern half of Allen in 1848). Waynesfield, like Harrod designated a village, was only slightly larger with a 1930 population of 561.

In Waynesfield, Carl and Florence Meyers began their life together living on the second floor of a two-story house that was owned by the telephone company. In due time they had two children. Both children were born at home, Charles on March 22, 1937 and his younger sister Shirley on July 6, 1938. When not working at the local sawmill Carl loved to hunt; he also taught his son how to hunt, holding the shotgun while Charles pulled the trigger to bag his first rabbit. With Carl's eight grown siblings, along with Florence's six brothers and sisters (Lula, Myrtle, and Elsie were her sisters; Robert, Lloyd, and Carl were her brothers), they always had relatives to visit and they were a tight-knit family. Family gatherings, frequently at Florence's sister Lula's farm, always included fruit picked from the trees, chickens from the farm, and Carl's homemade ice cream. Working at the sawmill had limited potential for future advancement, so in 1943 the Meyers family moved to Lima (in Allen County) where Carl was employed by Lima City Bus Lines, Inc., driving a bus in the city's public transportation system. The next year, Florence began working at Westinghouse as a motor winder; as a woman working in a factory during World War II, she was a "Rosie the Riveter."

While Carl and Florence Meyers worked, raised their family, and generally enjoyed their lives, international diplomacy brought the world to the brink of war. The conflict broke out in Asia in 1937 and Europe in 1939, and America had to prepare for the prospect of fighting in yet another world war. One of the most important preparations the country had to make was the building of an army; when war broke out in Europe, September 1, 1939, President Roosevelt "proclaimed a limited national emergency and authorized increases in Regular Army and National Guard enlisted strengths to 227,000 and 235,000, respectively."[1] Steps had to be taken to strengthen the armed forces if America was to be prepared to fight. Perhaps it was time for Congress to consider conscription.

The United States had passed conscription laws only twice prior to World War II, during the Civil War and World War I. In both of those cases, conscription was enacted only after America was a belligerent. During the Civil War, draft laws passed in the U.S. Congress in March 1863 and the Confederate Congress in April 1862, and in World War I, Congress enacted conscription in May 1917, a month after declaring war. In 1940, America considered enacting the country's first peacetime draft. And if a peacetime draft was not controversial enough, this discussion took place in the middle of a presidential election campaign. Both candidates, Democrat Franklin Roosevelt and Republican Wendell Willkie, came out in favor of the draft, so the issue played only a minor role in the campaign. After much national discussion Congress passed a conscription bill and President Roosevelt signed it on September 16, 1940.

The Selective Training and Service Act of 1940 was one of the important steps in mobilizing for the possibility of entering the war as a combatant. The legislation called for all men between the ages of 21 and 35 to register for the draft on the appointed day, which was October 16, 1940. Congress placed limits on the number of men who could be called up (900,000 per year), how long they could serve (1 year), and where they could be deployed (not outside the Western Hemisphere). The legislation also created local draft boards to supervise conscription; these boards had wide latitude in granting exemptions and deferments. Violation of the law could result in the punishment of up to five years imprisonment and a fine of up to $10,000.[2]

Congress revised and amended the selective service bill several times over the next few years, as America entered the war and the country's manpower needs changed. Among the significant revisions were the lowering of the draft age to 18, making a draftee's service "for the duration of the war," and the exemption of agricultural workers and those employed in the war industries. Married men and fathers were also exempted from the draft, exemptions that were removed when it was discovered that men were getting married and becoming fathers for the express purpose of evading the draft. This action brought up a troubling question—what about those men who were fathers before the exemption was written into the law, those men who did not become fathers specifically to avoid the draft? These men, who were called Pre-Pearl Harbor fathers, were virtually untouchable at the beginning of the war. As the country's manpower needs increased, especially in 1944, Pre-Pearl Harbor fathers were drafted, and many served as riflemen in combat zones.[3]

Once the Selective Service Bill passed and was signed by the president, Registration Day, or "R-Day" as it was called in 1940, was established for October 16, 1940. On that day, all men in America between the ages of 21 and 35 had to register for the draft. Those men who might be out of town on R-Day were told to show up at the county courthouse wherever they were and register there; the registration forms and information would be sent to their local draft boards. On registration day, all registrants completed a questionnaire comprised of 11 basic questions, such as name, address, telephone number, age, employer, and others. Later, those men completed a more detailed questionnaire that was mailed to their home. Upon completion of the registration process, each man was assigned a registration number. Each man in a draft district was assigned a different number, but across the country there were thousands of men with the same number. A fairly common greeting between men of draft age in the fall of 1940 was "What's your number?"

Another phenomenon of the draft process, and one that became controversial, was the local draft board. Members of the local boards had significant authority over who got drafted and who did not. State governors recommended potential board members to President Roosevelt, who then made the appointments. Board members were federal officials and usually prominent men who possessed a great deal of knowledge about the men of draft age in their community. World War I veterans were highly desirable for service on these local boards, since they would be asking young men to do what they had already done—fight for their country. Also, it seemingly would be much more difficult for a man in the 1940s to request an exemption from a veteran. Sergeant Alvin York, arguably America's most famous World War I hero, served on his local draft board in Franklin County, Tennessee. Members of these boards earned the enmity of many men whose request for an exemption was denied; the boards themselves became lightning rods to many potential draftees.

Prior to Registration Day, the local draft board for Auglaize County, Ohio was formed, and in early October 1940, five men were recommended to Ohio Governor John W. Bricker. These five men were: Colonel Roy Layton, formerly Ohio's adjutant general during World War I; Albert M. Koch, mayor of St. Mary's Township; Ferd F. Eversman, music instructor from New Knoxville; Julius Woehrmeyer, dairy farmer from Minster; and E.C. Weygandt, funeral director from Waynesfield. Later in the month, Mont Young, former St. Mary's city auditor was selected as clerk to the board, and Harold Goetz, former Wapakoneta common pleas court bailiff, was added as assistant clerk.[4] The board established its office in the county courthouse. This board had great influence over which men from Auglaize County, Ohio served in the U.S. Armed Services if war came to America.

On Registration Day, October 16, 1940, Carl Meyers was living in the Waynesfield district of Auglaize County. On the appointed day, he made his way to his voting precinct and duly registered with selective services (in Auglaize County, men reported to their voting precincts to register). Having celebrated his 30th birthday just two months prior to registering, Meyers was likely one of the older men who made himself available for the draft. He was assigned registration number 2288. All told 2,952 men registered in Auglaize County on October 16, 1940, 48 of them from Waynesfield. Of that number, 112 forms were sent to Columbus, as those men lived elsewhere; an additional 35 Auglaize County men registered somewhere else. Therefore, a total of 2,875 men from Auglaize County registered.[5] The 1940 census return for Auglaize County listed 28,037 residents, so over 10% of the county's population registered for the draft.

By the end of October 1940, the first men were drafted and inducted for service, and this group included about 100 men from Auglaize County. Carl Meyers was not included in this initial group of draftees, probably for several reasons. First, he was 30 years old at that time, and selective service was not necessarily interested in conscripting men of that age during peacetime. Second, Meyers had two children, which put him in that Pre-Pearl Harbor fathers classification. Men of draft age who had children prior to the attack on Pearl Harbor and the resulting declaration of war were virtually untouchable to selective services in 1940 and the first few years of the war. By early 1944, only 161,000 Pre-Pearl Harbor fathers had been drafted, so Meyers was relatively safe from the draft. For now.

In the meantime, in 1943, Meyers moved with his family from Waynesfield to Lima, Ohio, in Allen County. Allen County had a larger population, which numbered 73,303 in the 1940 census, and on R-Day 8,430 Allen County men registered with selective services.[6] Upon moving to Lima, Meyers was employed by the Lima City Bus Lines, Inc., driving a bus in the city's public transportation system. In the selective service classification,

Meyers's occupation was listed as "skilled chauffeurs and drivers, bus, taxi, truck, and tractor."

While the Meyers family contemplated a move to Lima, the Japanese attacked Pearl Harbor on December 7, 1941, and the country was drawn into yet another world conflict. His age and status as a Pre-Pearl Harbor father probably combined to keep Meyers out of the draft, though his status as a father was seemingly a more significant factor than his age. By the end of 1943, selective services and local draft boards went out of their way to keep fathers out of uniform. One study uses the term "shielded" in describing fathers and the draft.[7] By late 1943, local draft boards failed to meet quotas and underdrafted in order to avoid conscripting fathers. In the final months of that year, local draft boards succeeded in providing only two-thirds of the number of draftees requested. America simply was not prepared to send fathers into battle, and the general public agreed with this policy. In early 1944, a poll indicated that by a three-to-one majority, Americans preferred that single women be drafted before men with children.[8] Draft boards also began to conscript 18-year-olds before fathers. Unfortunately for those fathers, they could not remain out of the draft for long, as a manpower crunch hit the armed services in 1944. At the beginning of that year, fathers made up only 6% of those conscripted; by April 1944, they constituted over 50%. Carl E. Meyers from the Buckeye State was one of those called up in the 1944 manpower crunch.

In the first few months of 1944, selective service and the local draft boards stepped up their conscription of eligible men. Those men who were drafted received their first notification that they were selected when they received an order to report for a preinduction physical examination. These letters began with the salutation "Greeting," and draft-age men universally called this correspondence the "greetings." Men who received this letter knew it was only a matter of time, especially in 1944, before they donned an Army uniform. The physical examination was a one-day event, a kind of cattle-call of men lined up to be seen by various physicians. Because they were often done at remote locations that required the men to be transported some distance, the soon-to-be soldiers were ordered to report early in the morning. Many men who were not familiar with the process believed they were immediately going off to the Army, and brought their own weapons with them to the physical examination. After being seen by the doctors, the men returned home and awaited word on the results. Frequently, those who passed their physical were sworn into the Army right then and there, and were technically on furlough as they awaited their official notice of induction. Within a few days of the physical exam, the men received notification that they were deemed physically fit for military service or rejected as physically unfit. Being certified as physically fit was a fair indication that one could expect to be officially inducted into one of the branches of the military, and the registrant should begin making appropriate preparations.

Carl Meyers received his order to report for his preinduction physical in early February 1944. His order was dated February 3, and he was to report to the courthouse at Wapakoneta, Ohio (Wapakoneta was the county seat of Auglaize County) at 6:15a.m. on February 14, 1944. The notice also informed him that if he believed he had some "disqualifying defect," he should appear before the local draft board on or before February 7. There is no record that Meyers made such a claim. Being a reasonably fit man, Meyers could probably expect to be classified as physically fit, and the selective service system duly notified him of that shortly after being examined. Often, after passing the physical, those declared fit were assigned their serial number and took the oath of induction. For all intents and purposes they were soldiers now, going home on furlough. Carl Meyers, having passed his physical examination and taken the oath, could expect to receive his official induction notice within a short time.

Just a few short weeks after his physical examination, Carl Meyers received his Order to Report for Induction. Dated March 10, 1944, he was to report to the courthouse at Wapakoneta on March 21, the day before his son's seventh birthday. Early in the war, many places held send-off ceremonies for the men going off to the Army, but in 1944 the residents of Wapakoneta likely did not gather to see the men off. The March 21 edition of the *Wapakoneta Daily News* noted that "Thirty-four Auglaize county young men left this morning for Columbus for final induction into the U.S. Army."[9] The article listed all 34 men and their hometowns, including Carl Edgar Meyers of Waynesfield. From there, Meyers traveled to an Army reception center, Fort Benjamin Harrison in Lawrence, Indiana, northeast of Indianapolis. The reception center was where the new soldiers were processed, and the length of their stay varied, depending on numerous circumstances. Meyers was at Fort Benjamin Harrison for the week of March 21-28. At the reception centers, the men received their uniforms, more physical examinations and shots, and they took several written tests, including the Army General Classification Test (AGCT), to determine their placement in the Army.

By March 22, his second day at Fort Benjamin Harrison and his son's birthday, Meyers was taking the various Army tests. After taking the tests, he had interviews with Army personnel, and the result was that Meyers believed he would be placed in the Transportation Division. This made sense considering his prewar occupation. However, with the manpower crunch in early 1944, the Army needed infantry riflemen more than motor pool personnel. In addition to taking tests, Meyers received inoculations while at Fort Harrison. On March 23 he reported that he received his uniforms—"a whole sack full," and spent a fair amount of time marking his clothing with his initials and serial number. Another task Meyers completed in his first few days as a soldier was to fill out the paperwork for the $10,000 insurance policy the Army provided. The men at the reception centers got their first experiences of life in the Army, and it was an adjustment for all of them. Meyers wrote that he could not get used to not talking back to the boss when given an order, that he was expected to follow the order and not say anything about it. Another adjustment was the food. Five days after arriving at Fort Harrison Meyers wrote that "the eats haven't been so bad"; he reported having ham, potatoes, cabbage, lettuce, and pears that day, and that he thought he had put on a little weight. After a week at Fort Benjamin Harrison, Meyers was on a train headed to Camp Fannin, Texas for his basic training.

By the time Meyers boarded his train for Texas, the Army training program had evolved considerably. In the first couple years of the war, roughly 1941-1943, training was focused on large-unit training, usually at the division level. The Army division was the basic fighting unit, so it made sense to train soldiers on that level. The decision had already been made to limit the U.S. Army to 90 divisions, so when that threshold was reached, the training was changed. With no additional divisions being created, new soldiers were trained to be replacements for casualties in existing units that were already in the field seeing combat. By 1944, basic training was conducted at facilities called Replacement Training Centers (RTC), of which Camp Fannin was one.

The goal of the training program at the RTC was to prepare the replacement soldier to be added to a unit at the front seamlessly and for him to be an effective part of that unit. According to the Army's official history of infantry training, "The mission of these training centers was to provide a steady flow of trained men to tactical units..."[10] These men, generally known as replacements, received a broad training at the RTCs, and it was necessary to avoid narrow specialized training. The Army study explained that the goal was "to provide replacements sufficiently well trained so that they could be placed in units without unduly disrupting either the training or the combat efficiency of the unit involved."[11] In July 1943, the War Department increased the length of the replacement training program from 13 weeks to 17 weeks, effective August 1943. The additional weeks were devoted to small-unit training, such as company- and battalion-level, and two weeks of continuous field exercises. Also added to the training program in 1943 was a series of "special battle courses" designed to make the training more realistic—an infiltration course, close combat course, and a village fighting course. These were to give the trainees more experience under battle conditions. The added realism and the two-week field exercise program should prepare the replacements to go right into battle upon their arrival in a theater of operation.

Beyond those general guidelines, the various Mobilization Training Program (MTP) plans outlined the men's training regimen. The MTPs were written by War Department officials and generally consisted of two parts, one that outlined the training program in general and another that included a more specific breakdown of those activities. The initial MTP for infantry training was a 13-week program, which was lengthened to 17 weeks in 1943, as already mentioned. For infantry, five weeks was devoted to basic or general training, and the remainder on more specialized areas, such as marksmanship. Other aspects, such as drill, physical training, inspection, and marching, took place throughout the entire program. In addition, the trainees received classroom-setting instruction in military courtesy, discipline, sanitation, first aid, the Articles of War, along with other military protocol. The men also heard lectures on Army organization and the progress of the war to-date; they may have even viewed one or more of Frank Capra's *Why We Fight* films. This was the basic training program that Private Carl Meyers followed at Camp Fannin in the spring and summer of 1944.

Camp Fannin was located nine miles north of Tyler, the county seat of Smith County in east Texas, and within a 25-mile radius were Gladewater, Kilgore, and Longview. The camp was situated on 15,000 rolling acres surrounded by east Texas oil fields, and was named after Colonel James Walker Fannin, who distinguished himself in the Texas War for Independence in 1836. Camp Fannin was dedicated as an Army Replacement Training Center in March 1943, and by December 1945, over 200,000 soldiers received their training there. Men assigned there were issued a Handbook of Information that outlined the camp, their upcoming training program, and included a map of the camp. These handbooks were also available to be mailed home to family.

Meyers boarded a train on March 28, 1944 and headed for Texas, although he had only a vague idea of where he was going. He noted that three friends from Ohio were also on the train, Paul Spillman, Leonard ("Shorty") Pyles, and Bob Styles. Spillman and Pyles were, like Meyers, Pre-Pearl Harbor fathers. Those four spent as much time as they could together during their training. Meyers narrated his trip to Texas in a letter home, and noted that they arrived at Camp Fannin on March 30. Upon arrival, the trainees were told that they would not get to go home for 17 weeks, which was the length of the training program. Meyers was assigned to Company B, 68th Training Battalion, and drill and other exercises began immediately. Historian Lee Kennett has found a surviving training schedule for Camp Fannin from late 1944, and while Meyers was not there that time of the year, his typical day was probably similar:

> First call (and not reveille) was sounded at 5:55 A.M.; reveille and its roll call came ten minutes later. By 6:20 the soldiers had washed, dressed, made their bunks, and fallen in for the five-minute march to the mess hall. After a twenty-minute stay there they marched back to their barracks; they then policed the area, prepared their equipment, and made the forty-minute march to the train-

ing site, where they pursued scheduled training activities from 8:00 A.M. until 5:30 P.M., the nine and a half hours broken only for the midday meal, which the Army called dinner. By the time the men marched back to barracks, then made the trip to supper and back, it was 7:00. The working day was not really over, however: There was still mail call and announcements, housekeeping chores, fatigue details, and the cleaning of equipment. The schedule allotted thirty minutes for showering and preparing for bed, and at 9:45 the lights went out. The training day could thus take almost sixteen hours. In addition, there were occasional night-training problems, weekend cleaning details known as "G.I. parties," and KP duties (the latter with a wakeup time of 4:55 A.M.); training time lost while on guard or KP duty was to be made up during "free time" in the evening--from 9:20 to 9:45.[12]

This is probably close to the schedule Meyers followed while at Camp Fannin, though the men typically did not train on Sundays. It was definitely a big adjustment from civilian life, but within a couple of weeks the rigors became more routine and the men took pride in their training.

Private Meyers was a frequent correspondent while he endured the hardships that were his basic training. From March 22, 1944, his second day at Fort Benjamin Harrison, to July 24, 1944 Meyers wrote 76 letters home to his wife Florence.[13] He typically wrote every day or every other day, and rarely did as many as three days lapse without correspondence. No letters to him survived.

Throughout the letters Meyers wrote from training, several themes were revealed, most of which were common for soldiers away from home (during any conflict).[14] Most soldiers' letters (again, during any conflict) included general gossip and chit-chat, and the two predominant themes in this correspondence were Army life and talk of home. Soldiers who are away from home always like to receive mail, and Private Meyers was no different. In his April 25, 1944 letter he wrote, "It really helps to keep a fellows spirit up to get a little Mail each day." In virtually every letter, he commented on the letters he received, or did not receive; he was at Camp Fannin for two days when he mentioned that it had been a week since he received mail. On several occasions he jokingly asked his wife Florence if her arm was broken, and when he had not written for several days, he made the same joke about himself. Receiving and writing letters was the most common topic in his correspondence.

Soldiers who are sent far from home for their training often compare the geography, landscape, and weather to home, and note how far away they are from home. Particularly early in his time at Camp Fannin, Meyers commented on the Texas weather and how flat the landscape was. On the train en route to Texas he described the landscape, and by April 1 he estimated that he was 1200 miles from home. The heat in Texas in early April was such that the men were told they could take off their shirts during drills, probably something that would not be done at home in Ohio during that time of year. Another geographical observation Meyers made was the insects the trainees encountered while out training, especially mosquitoes and chiggers (although he called them "jiggers").

Meyers also reported his non-military activities. The Army scheduled shows of all kinds to keep the new soldiers occupied when not training, and Meyers noted in 15 different letters that he and his buddies attended them. When time permitted, soldiers were allowed to go into the nearest town, which in this case was Tyler, Texas. Periodically, Meyers went into town, and on several occasions had his picture taken to send home, which he mentioned in seven letters. On one trip to Tyler he and his hometown friend Paul Spillman had their photo taken in a cowboy outfit. While in town, Meyers tried to find little gifts to send home to his wife and children, especially when he missed birthdays and his anniversary. One gift he sent to his wife was what he called "pillow tops"; these were pillow shams and they were adorned with Army and Camp Fannin motifs. Soldiers in basic training tried to maintain a semblance of civilian life whenever they could.

The second most common topic in Meyers's correspondence was his training; he never failed to report what he and his fellow trainees were doing. In these letters, one can grasp the basic outline of the soldiers' training and what skills the Army expected them to acquire—the elements of being an infantryman. Early letters told of physical training and learning how to roll their packs, pitch their tents, marching, basic drill exercises, and cleaning their rifles. After that, the men experienced bayonet practice, grenade training, and how to properly fire their rifles and machine guns. They followed that up with mortar and heavy weapons training, and at the end of their program conducted field problems, or night problems. In these "problem" training exercises, the men were away from camp for several days at a time and bivouacked out in the field. The training program prepared the men to be combat riflemen.

Throughout his time at Camp Fannin, Meyers reported on how he fared, particularly his success in rifle training. He qualified as a sharpshooter, something he mentioned in seven of his letters; he even signed two or three as "sharpshooter." In rifle qualification, the trainees shot at targets from different distances in four different positions: 100 yards standing, 200 yards kneeling, 300 yards sitting, and 500 yards prone. There were three levels of marksmanship: expert was the highest, sharpshooter was next, and marksman was the lowest. For qualifying at any of those levels, the recruit received a badge, or medal, that he wore on his uniform. Meyers's medal for scoring as a sharpshooter was in the shape of a Maltese cross with a target superimposed over the center of the cross. Winning any kind of recognition always helped the men's morale and it must have done the same for Meyers, especially when receiving his sharpshooter medal. In his rifle training, Meyers

Paul Spillman, Leonard "Shorty" Pyles, Carl Meyers, and Ernest Numbers (left to right), taken while they were in basic training at Camp Fannin, 1944. Photo in possession of the authors.

may have been provided with a copy of the little book *How to Shoot the U.S. Army Rifle*, which The Infantry Journal, Inc. first published in 1943. This training manual, 122 pages long, detailed the proper way to fire an Army rifle. It also offered its readers sage advice (which doubled as propaganda): "The last war proved that if you hit a German in the right place with a caliber .30 rifle bullet, he falls over dead. This is also true in this war. It applies,

Paul Spillman and Carl Meyers had their photograph taken in cowboy outfits in Tyler, Texas while in basic training at Camp Fannin, 1944. Photo in possession of the authors.

moreover, to Japs as well as Nazis."[15] In addition to chronicling his progress in the training program, he reported on his soldierly appearance—on April 1 he wrote that his uniform fit was "not bad," and that he had gotten a "G.I. Haircut." Meyers was quickly becoming a soldier.

Two topics of keen interest to Meyers and all of his fellow trainees were how long they had left in basic training, and where they were going to be sent after completing the program. In seven of his letters, Meyers mentioned how many weeks remained. The rumor also circulated that the program might be reduced from 17 weeks to 12, and he duly noted those. The men's post-training destination was seemingly more important to Meyers than some others because of his age and status as a Pre-Pearl Harbor father. He was acutely aware of all of the rumors about where the older men would be sent. Among the stories he heard and passed on were that the Army was not even taking the old men, they would be put on reserve (he heard this rumor multiple times), no Pre-Pearl Harbor fathers would be sent overseas, and that no man over 30 would be sent overseas. The rumors were groundless, and all trainees regardless of age or status served in the capacity for which they were trained.

One person Meyers brought up several times, and not in a complimentary manner, was a man from home named Duncan. Meyers seems to blame him specifically (and personally) for not getting him an exemption or deferment from the draft. From the context of the letters Duncan was seemingly either a supervisor or officer at the bus company where Meyers worked before being drafted or a member of the local draft board (supervisor at the bus company seems more likely). In his June 23 letter, he flatly stated that Duncan "could have got me a Deferment if he would have tried." Two months earlier, in his April 23 letter, he said it more crudely when he wrote, "I guess I didn't Suck Duncan's Ass enough." Meyers certainly had bitter feelings for Duncan.

Even though Meyers and his fellow trainees were focused on their training, they were aware of the war being fought overseas. In two letters, Meyers mentioned the fighting. In his May 8, 1944 letter, he explained that War Department news was read to them every day. Later, on June 6, Meyers acknowledged his awareness that the Normandy Invasion (D-Day) had begun: "Well they finally got the Invasion started..." The recruits were certainly kept aware of the war's progress, even if they did not know what part they were to play in it. The recruits, like the men already fighting, wanted the conflict over, as Meyers expressed in his May 21 letter: "I sure will be glad when this dam thing is over..."

On a lighter note, Meyers passed along a poem one of the men wrote about life in the Army. The poem was titled "Army-Life" and was a humorous, and sometimes crude, take on what the men were experiencing. It seems to be a standard piece that was probably widely circulated in training centers around the country. It was lengthy, 34 stanzas long, and included names of men in the training company (the names, of course, could be changed with each new group of trainees).

By the end of July 1944, Meyers and his compatriots completed their basic training and went home on furlough awaiting orders to a theater of action. He had survived his 17-week training program, turned himself into a bona fide soldier, and had earned a sharpshooter medal. After attending parties to celebrate the end of basic training, Meyers boarded a train for Lima, Ohio, and a reunion with his family.

Carl Meyers at home on leave after completing basic training with his wife Florence (right), his sister-in-law Elsie (back), and an unidentified family friend (left), 1944. Photo in possession of the authors.

NOTES

1. *American Military History*, Revised Edition (Washington, D.C.: Center of Military History, 1989), 418.
2. For the wording of the bill see *U.S. Statutes at Large*, 1939-1941, volume 54, part 1, 885-889.
3. For good discussions of the draft, see Lee Kennett, *G.I.: The American Soldier in World War II* (Norman: University of Oklahoma Press, 1997), 3-41 and George Q. Flynn, *Lewis B. Hershey, Mr. Selective Service* (Chapel Hill: University of North Carolina Press, 1985), 67-134.
4. *Wapakoneta Daily News*, October 2, 1940.
5. For these numbers, see *Wapakoneta Daily News*, October 17, 21, 1940.
6. *Lima News*, October 17, 1940.
7. Lee Kennett, *G.I.*, 22.

8. Ibid.
9. *Wapakoneta Daily News*, March 21, 1944.
10. Robert R. Palmer, Bell I. Wiley, and William R. Keast, *The Procurement and Training of Ground Combat Troops* (Washington, D.C.: Government Printing Office, 1948), 369.
11. Ibid., 381.
12. Lee Kennett, *G.I.*, 53.
13. He may have written more, but 76 survived.
14. For World War II soldiers, see Lee Kennett, *G.I.*, especially 42-65 and Gerald Linderman, *The World Within War: America's Combat Experience in World War II* (Cambridge: Harvard University Press, 1997), especially 303-306; for Civil War soldiers, see Bell I. Wiley, *The Life of Johnny Reb* (Indianapolis: Bobbs-Merrill, 1943), especially 192-216 and *The Life of Billy Yank* (Indianapolis: Bobbs-Merrill, 1952), especially 45-65.
15. *How to Shoot the U.S. Army Rifle* (Washington, D.C.: The Infantry Journal, Inc., 1943), 9.

Chapter Two

The Letters from Basic Training

3-22-44
Fort Ben. Ind.

Dear Florence-All,
    Have got about 1 hour off between tests so will try to Drop you a few lines. Arrived last night about 6:00 A.M. Walked about 2 miles from where we got off of the train to camp. We haven't got our uniforms yet, expect to get them this afternoon. Well how are you getting along? Fine I hope. I am getting along O'K. only would rather be home. We haven't received our serial number, as yet. If you need me in any emergency you can get in touch with Co. A, Barr. 618. That is where I am sleeping I think we will get settled down today Then I will write my full address.
    Must close for now.
    With lots of Love,
    P.V.T. Carl Meyers-Co. A, Barr. 618

Mar-[2]3-44
Fort-Ben.

Dear Mom-Kids-In Laws,
    Well I am a Full Pledged Soldier Now. Just a (Buck PVT). How is everybody back home now. I am feeling pretty good. We just got shot in the arm about an hour ago. Got my clothes today. A whole sack full. 5 Pair Pants 6 Pr socks, 4 Shirts 3 jackets and coats, 1 overcoat-1 Raincoat, 3 Caps, 2 Neckties 3 handkerchiefs, a Tin hat and a wool cap, 3 suits of summer underwear-2 suits of winter, I think that is about all. Well folks I guess we will get done signing up to morrow. I hope so. All we have done so far is run from one office to another. Then stand from 1 to three hours. Has Steve[1]

heard anything yet? And how are you getting along. Well we got our numbers-and you can put it on the letters and I will get them. Well we have to go to a show to night and it is about time so must close for now. Oh yes my clothes should be coming home in a couple of days. Say could you send me about 4 clothes hangers.

With Love-Wishes to all,
PVT Carl Meyers

Mar-24-44
Fort-Ben.

Dear Mom-All,

Just a line to let you know that I lived after my shot. My arm got Pretty sore last night, but it is better now. I had a Fire watch[2] last night, 2 hours from 3 to 5. It wasn't bad. We had to get up at 4:30 anyway. Say you try and be home Sunday night about 8:00 if we are still here I may try to call you. How are you and the kids getting along.

Must close with Love,
PVT Meyers

Mar-24-44
Fort-Ben.

Dear Wife-Kids,

Well as it is about an hour yet until bedtime I will try to scribble a few more lines. We had it pretty soft today, but I have been working all evening in the barrack's putting my Initial and Number on my clothes It was a hell of a job. We had to do it with an Indelable pencil. Well I Don't think we will be here very much longer. Thier are so many new men coming in all of the time they have to send the others out as soon as they are done testing them. We had our last interview today. I think the way they talked I will be in the Transportation Division. I sent you some papers today you just keep them I guess, it is the papers we made out for the Insurance and allottments. They Didn't say anything about bond's.

Say them clothe's hangers I wrote about, you don't need to send them now. Spillman and I went down to the Red Cross today and got some. When I get settled I would like to have 2 or 3 wooden ones, if you can find them for me. When you write to me here be sure to put (Co. A) on my address. I got a card from Etta[3] today. Sure glad to hear that Dad is feeling better. How is Charles' Pox has Shirley got them yet. Well it is about time to turn in so must close for now.

With Lots of Love and Good Luck to all tell Steve-Elsie-Dick[4] Hello,
PVT Meyers

Mar-26-44
Fort Ben.

Dear Mom-Kiddies-All-

Well it is Monday noon. Just got done eating chow. Had Baked ham, Fried potatoes, Boiled Cabbage, Lettuce, and Pear's. So far the eats haven't been so bad. I think that I am putting on a little weight. Not quite as bad as Steve yet.

Well you ask me how I liked this army life. I know that I have to stay so I am getting along O.K. only thing I cannot get used to not talking back to the (Boss) when they give an order they expect you to go ahead and do it, and not say anything about it. We are still on the same detail only we would call it a Job. We will get done with it this A.M. I don't know what will be next. K.P. I expect. Did Charles start back To school today? And how is Shirley getting along with the Chicken Pox. Well Mom I want to write to Dad-Etta so I think I had better close for now. If I get time to night may write some more. say I almost forgot when I called you last night they said we talked 11 minutes. It didn't seem more than about 4 or 5 to me. Well this is all for now,

Goodbye and good luck.
With Love. Best Wishes
PVT C.E. Meyers 35247984
Co A. Brks 618
Fort Ben. Harrison
Ind.

Mar-28-44
Enroute from
Fort Ben to ——

Dear Mom-All,

We are on our way don't know where. Lone Star State of Texas I think, we left Fort Ben at 2:20 P.M. 3-28-44-got to Indianapolis about 2:45-left at 3:15 ate chow at 5:30-read a little after it got dark. Arrived in St. Louis Missouri at 8:30-I went to bed while they were stopped their. Dam near froze to death during the night had an upper berth all to myself. got up at 5:30 A.M. ate chow at 6:15 and now we are in Arkansas. When we got up this morning we were only 275 miles from St. Louis. They had to stop and take some cars off during the night some of the troops was going to a different place. We are now stopped over at a little one horsed town named Watts Ark. They are changing train crew's. They have changed engines once. We stopped at Camp Crowder Mo. This morning and they got a new supply of water and Grub. I hope it is good. We had a good supper last night. Breakfast this morn. Wasn't so hot. Say I almost forgot to tell you Paul Spillman is cooking on this trip Shorty Pyles and Bob Styles[5] are in the car behind the one I am in. They are Playing Poker. I don't think I will play any. Well we are on our way again. This sure is a hell of a Country. I wouldn't live out here for the best farm I have saw yet.

Well Folks I have rested a little while now so will write some more. Just saw some Dandelion's out in bloom, the peach trees are all out to. it is 11:45 A.M. and we haven't had chow yet. expecting it anytime. We have been in Oklahoma for quite awhile. We Passed through the town where that Baby Faced Floyd the gangster used to live. Tell Steve that Jimmy Bivins the colored fighter went to Fort Ben on the same train I did. He hit a Sgt. over the head with a broom stick. The Sgt. called him a black Boy. I didn't hear what they did to him. I saw him several time's. say if you can't read this let me know, and I will come home and read it for you. HA. HA. It sure is a Job trying to write on this train sometimes you can see the back of the train. Well it is about time to eat so will sign off until afterwards. I do hope it is good and lots of it. Well chow is over it wasn't so bad-had tenderized Ham, Green bean's, diced Potatoes, Hot Chocolate Bread and butter and each one got a big apple. Well I saw some Lilacs out in bloom awhile ago. it is getting kind of warm. My long undies is getting hot. It isn't quite as hilly as it was back the way a few miles, but it is still to rough for me. They are pulling this train with a Diesel engine, they sure are high balling it now. Tell Elsie I just saw a Mule, and it made me homesick to see her. Thier sure are a lot of them down through here. Boy am I getting tired of riding. My back is beginning to hurt. Thier is a bunch of Kentuckians in this Car they seem to be right home down here. Well we are in Heavener Okla. 1:15 P.M. Stopped Don't know what for. We have to stop for everything. Well I think I will Rest awhile as I am getting kind of sleepy. More later. Well I had better write a little More. I just took a little nap then washed and shaved and brushed my teeth, we are now in Arkansas again. It is getting warmer all the time the grass is pretty green and the trees are coming out in leaves. We are getting pretty close to Fort Smith Ark. It sure as Hell is hilly. We crossed a Mt. Range a while ago. I suppose you will have My New address before I get to Camp. They had us fill out card's to send to our Home town News Paper before we left they put our new address on it and mail it out. Well it is a little Past 4:00 so I think I will quit until after chow. If we go Much farther it will take you all day to read this Mess. Well Mom It is 5:20 P.M. Mar. 29-we are at Dequeen Ark. Stopped again I don't know what is the Matter, we have to stop for every hitching Post, and sidetrack for all the hand car's. We are only 5 Miles from the Texas State line it is Chow time More later. Well Chow is over. Feel better. We are in Texas it sure is nice. It has leveled off, and I think Martin Croler the Crazy engineer is on duty, he sure is taking us a ride. The Porter just said it was 150 Miles from here to the Camp where we are going it sure has been a long ride. I suppose we will arrive about 1:30 or 2:00 oclock in the morning, then get up at 5:00. Well how is everybody back home? Fine I hope. have you heard from My Dad lately and how is he getting along. I am afraid if he should happen to Pass away Now I wouldn't get to come home. It is a hell of a long ways home.

They told us at Fort Ben if any thing like that happened the Red Cross would lend us Money to come home. Well this is about all right Now. We have been stopped for awhile but we are going again Now. I will have to look or I Might Miss something, more later.

Well here it is Mar. 30 1:00 P.M. just had chow. It was pretty good we didn't get off the train until this morn about 7:00 oclock, we got into Camp about 1:30 A.M. but we were in bed and they left us sleep until morning. The Sargent told us that Nobody would get to go home for at least 17 weeks. boy that is along time if you ask me. Well it is about time to fall out for drill and I don't know My address so will quit for a while. Well it is almost time to go to bed so will write a few lines again. We had a little drill this A.M. only about 1 hour, then we had chow. After our chow Shorty, Paul and I went to the P.X. it is a Restaurant. You can buy most anything you Need here cigarettes $.13 a Pack. Not bad. Then we came back and Shaved-and took a Shower. It sure is Nice out here, It is real flat you can see for a long ways, and all you can see is yellow sand. Well I think I had better close and get in bed because I suppose to morrow will be pretty tough. I think I will like it better here then I did at Fort Ben. only it is so dam far from home. Well Mom take good Care of yourself and the kiddies until I get back, and I hope I won't be to long. With Lots of Love and best Wishes. Your loving husband and Dad,

    PVT Carl E. Meyers 35247984
    Co. B, 68.-B.N.-14-Regt.
    Camp. Fannin-Texas

Mar-31-44
Camp. Fannin Texas

Dear Mom-All,

Will scribble a few lines before the lights go out it is only about 20 minutes yet. We went to the show[6] tonight, it wasn't so hot. We didn't see it all. Say Mom if you want to, and need it send some more of them bonds in and get them cashed, they are going to take $6.25 a month for bonds. We didn't have to but will make you wish you had, so we took them out. It is pretty hot here in the day time but it gets cool at night. last night they only gave us one cover it was a Furniture Pad and I dam near froze to death this morn. Well the chow isn't so bad say let me know as soon as you get a check. I don't know if I will have enough money to last me until Pay day or not we

don't get any Pay until the last of April. Well it is about time for the lights to go out so I think I had better close, say do you ever write I haven't got a letter yet this week. good bye and good luck.
   With Lots of Love and best wishes,
   PVT Meyers

April-1-1944
Camp-Fannin-Texas

Dear Mom-All,
   Well it is Saturday night and all is quiet here. It sure is different then back home. Shorty-Paul and I went to the show to night. I had saw it before, Bob Hope in (Let's Face It) We saw it at the Ohio quite awhile ago.
   We were back at the Brks. at 9:00. Took a shower and am going to go to bed in a little while. We don't have to get up until 6:30 in the morn. We don't have to do anything on Sunday, just report for roll call at 8:00 in the morn and 1:00 P.M. then I suppose we will go to the show, they have a different show almost every night. What do you think? Shorty and I are going to Church in the morning. Then we are going to do some washing if we aren't to tired. Ha, Ha. Well if you haven't sent those hangers you don't need to they gave each of us seven when we got here.
   Well I suppose you will know by now that I am not very close to home till now. I guess it about 1200 miles to here, well my uniforms fit is not bad. Pants are a little long. One suit is only work clothes I guess we get another suit here it sure is nice and warm here in the day time but it gets kind of cool at night. They told us today that Monday when we drill we could take our Shirts off so you know it is kind of warm. Well we are getting pretty good eat's. The Srgt.-told us today that the training we get here in 17 week's we couldn't get any where else in a life time or it couldn't be bought. Well Mom I must close and get to bed will write more to morrow it is about time for the lights to go out. good bye and good Luck. With lots of Love,
   PVT MEYERS
   Say I forgot to tell you I got a G.I. Haircut. HA, HA.

April-2-44
Camp-Fannin-Texas

Dear Mom-All,
   Well Sunday we here about 4:00 oclock we haven't done a thing all day only eat and sit around. We did go to church this morning, when we got back from thier we went down to the Supply room and got our Rifles and Bayonet's. I think we are about fit out now except for another work suit.

Well Mom I did want to get you something for Easter but I don't know if I will get to it or not. We are restricted to the area around our Barracks, and you can't get any thing around here, only cigarettes, Pop, Candy, and Ice Cream. If we get turned loose in time this eve I want to go to the show, it is just across the street.

Say those two letters you wrote about the 27 March, I just got them Saturday P.M. You ask about Jack Melching. I never see him at all. I don't know if that Bill[7] is down here or not I haven't saw him. Since that Night I called you, you ask how much it cost, $1.74 for 11-minutes. One of the fellows here called to Ky. the other day talked 38 Minutes, reversed the charges. I'll bet that cost $10.00 at least. Well Mom I don't suppose I will call you for a while at least. I want to save all the Money I can so when it is time for My Furlough I can come home. I may have you send those bonds in and get them cashed, if I can't save enough money. That is if you don't have to before now. Say did Bus[8] get home? I hope so. I got two letters from you Sat. and one from Glenna.[9] I have got to write to Bus-Killian Glenna-Dad and Myrtle[10] this week. Well Mom I think I had better close and get ready for chow. Did you get the note I wrote while on the train that was some Trip. Good bye and best wishes. With Love and and Kisses to all.

PVT MEYERS

April-3-1944
Camp-Fannin

Dear Mom-All,

Well I just got your letter today saying that Steve had to report, sure am sorry to hear that. I would of gotten it sooner but it was at Fort Ben. and then it was forwarded here. It was Mailed in Lima March 29.

Well how is everything going back home? Fine I hope. I am getting along as well as could be expected. The chow here is better than it was at Fort Ben. We go to bed an hour later and get up an hour later so we don't get any more sleep, but so far it hasn't been so bad. it is just the idea of being away from home all of the time.

Shorty-and Bob Stiles are still in the same Brk's. Paul is in the one next to us. Shorty is on K.P. to day. I have been lucky so far but am expecting it any time. Shorty just came in he has been working since 4:00 A.M. it is now 7:30 he said he was about broke in to only had 15 minutes off all day.

We had it pretty easy all day they had us to the show[11] twice and gave us 4 or 5 lectures and we had 2 hours drill. We sat out side for the lectures. I got pretty cool but not to bad. Well Mom Shorty wants me to go over to the Post Exchange with him and I have to get some cigarettes so I think I had better close for now. Tell Steve to be sure and write to me when he gets settled

Down. Write and let me know how you are getting along and how everybody is. Shorty is ready so must close. With Lots of Love and Kisses and Best of Luck.

XXXXXX
PVT. MEYERS

April-4-44
Camp-Fannin

Dear Mom-All,

Well how is everybody now? Fine I hope. I am not feeling so good to night. We got a shot in each arm today and am on K.P. tomorrow. They fixed us around to-day. Thier isn't any of the boys from Waynesfield in my Brks. but Paul and I are in the same Platoon. He is on K.P. to. We have to get up at 4:30 in the morn.

We got some more clothes to day, 2 more work suits, another Pair of leggings, and a chain for our Dog tag's. They took us out in the field and had us roll our Pack. I still don't see how they get all of the stuff in it, 1 army Blanket-1 tent, Poles, Peg's mess kit-Towel-Toilet articles, and a little Pick to dig with, so I think I will have Plenty of clothes for a while. Say you couldn't come down and wash and Iron for me could you. I had to Sew on a button last Night on one of my wool shirts. I didn't do so hot, but I think it will Pass.

Say have you written since I Changed my address, all of the letters I have gotten so far have been to Fort Ben. I got those hangers to-day. Shorty hadn't got a letter since he has been in the army until to day he got seven. Boy was he tickled. Well it is about time for the lights to go out so will close until tomorrow nite. With Lots of Love and Kisses to all.

PVT. MEYERS

April-6-44
Camp-Fannin

Dear Mom-All,

Well I didn't have time to write last Night, so will wrote a little to day as I have time. They are really putting us through training Mostly physical exercise. Boy it is hard on My old Muscles. We are so sore in the Morning we can hardly get out of bed, but I guess we will get used to it. All the rest of them before us have. We have been having quite a bit of First Aid treatment and Physical Hygiene, also Pitching our tent and rolling our field Packs.

Well it is 9:00 P.M. we just got in from drill Practice. We had a Military test[12] from 6:00 to 6:30 have been out every since. I feel like going to bed. I got two letters from you today. Also the money. I wasn't expecting that and I didn't Need it. I have still got $13.00 of the Money I brought with Me Not

bad. Ha. Ha. How does Bus like the Navy? O.K. I hope. Say thier is a fellow in this Brks. by the Name of Morris from Wilmington, Ohio that used to have Cream-Egg's from Equity at Sardina he says that he knows Steve. Well Mom I think I had better close and get to bed. I have to shave yet. last we were out until late, and I had to shave and take a shower, so didn't have time to write. say after this when you write in the lower left hand corner on the envelope put PT.-1 as they are sending our Mail to the brks. Now. Thank's for the Card I sure hate it that I didn't get to send some home, but we haven't had time to get them. Well good-bye and Best Wishes. With lots of Love and Kisses.
    P.S. Tell the Kids I said Hellow,
    PVT. Meyers

April-8-44
Camp-Fannin

Dear Mom-All,
    Well it is Saturday Night and very quiet here. I just got this dated and Paul came and we went to the show, so will go on now. just got back it is only 9:30 don't you think I am getting awful good? I was going to write last but we were out drilling yesterday and got our guns full of sand. We didn't get them cleaned at 10:00 last Night, then had to Shave and take a shower, so did not get to write.
    I received a letter from dad today Noon and one from you this evening, sure am glad to receive them. The way dad-stated in his letter he is feeling some better. I sure hope he gets along O.K. for a while. I am going to write to him to morrow. If I have time. They are working us pretty hard. We get so sore and stiff we can hardly get out of bed, but I guess we will get used to it. Well Mom I think I will close and get some rest to night. We don't have to get up very early in the Morning. I will try and write again to morrow. As far as I know I haven't got anything to do I hope. Well Good bye and best wishes with lots of love and kisses.
    PVT. MEYERS-Tell the Kids Hello

April-9-1944
Camp-Fannin

Dear Mom-All,
    Recieved a letter from you today. Sure was glad to get it. It kind of helped to pass the time. Have been pretty busy all day. Ate Chow this Morn about 7:30 then came back and washed our dirty clothes and they were about all dirty. We start this week sending them to the laundry we can send all we want to only costs $1.50 per Month. I guess they take it out wether you send

it out or Not. They say when we get going good we won't have time to wash. We haven't hardly got time to shit Now. The Company Commander said that he didn't think any of us in this Platoon would ever go across. When they straightened us around the other day they put all of us old Men in one Platoon the youngest one here is 32. they split us up according to our age. You ask what Trg. Regt. was. that was only part of it. It all is I.R.T.C., which is Infantry Replacement (Training) Center.[13]

Well did you have a good time to day. I sure would like to have been home. But I guess I wont be for awhile. The way it figures out I should be home about time for our Birthdays. I hope. Say I got over to the Main P.X. Today. I got you a little Present. It wasn't Much, But about all you can get out here. Will try and do better the next time. They told us last Night we could go to Town last Night, But they wouldn't let Me go to the Town I wanted to go to, Lima Ohio Ha. Ha.

Say Mom will you look in the Telephone Book and get me Walter Kah's and Bob Walcutt's[14] address and send to me.

You wanted to know about coming down when school was out. It is 8 miles from here to Tyler Texas, and it isn't very big. The Sargent here said the hotels were engaged for Months ahead. If I go into town I will see what I can find out. I sure would like to see you and all the rest.

Say I almost forgot to tell you what we had for dinner (Turkey) Sweet Potatoes Corn, Head lettuce, Fruit Salad and Ice Cream. So far the eats have been pretty good here. Got weighed today, 182, so am about holding My own. Say you ask about My watch band you don't need to get one, as it is not working right, when I get to the Main P.O. I think I will send it home. Well Mom I think I had better sign off and go shave. I have got a little More work I want to do to night. I will try and get some write again every day. Maybe it be very Much but a little. Friday we didn't get done cleaning our guns until 10:00. Well Mom answer real soon and I will try and do the same. Must close with lots of love and Kisses to all. Good bye and Good luck.

PVT. Meyers

P.S. How is the Kids, and how is Charles getting along in school? Tell them I said Hello.

April-10-1944
Camp-Fannin

Dearest Mom-all,

Well it is Night again, and we are Restricted to the company area. We had a couple of test's this eve and because one windy ass hole talked None of us are allowed to go any place. I don't care Much, as I am going to take a shower and shave before I go to bed. We didn't have to work so hard today. But it is pretty hot in the day time. It rained a little this A.M. We had our

Rain Coats on and we realy got up a sweat. It gets kind of cool at Night but it isn't bad. I sleep right in front of a window, have it wide open all the time only use two blanket's, and that is plenty. It rains almost every day a little bit, but it don't last long. It take's a lot to Make it Muddy. It soon drys off.

A couple of the boys from Wapak.[15] just got a box of Candy and Cookies from home and they passed them around. That is the way they all do. They are Brothers here one is in the same Brks as me the other is in the Next. They get together quite a lot. Well Mom how is our Families getting along after thier operations? Fine I hope. What is the Matter with Elsie? (her head or the other end)-personal. Did you all have a good time Easter? We had a fairly good time. But would like to have been home. I got a letter from Aunt Etta and Uncle Walt Mowery to day also a Easter Card. How is My Dad getting along? Also your Dad. does he still go over to Hooker's[16] as Much as he did. I don't get around Much anymore. They sell Beer over at the P.X. But it is about like Dish Water. have only had one Bottle since I left Lima, sure would like to have a bout a Barrell. Well I think I had better close and get ready for bed. I can't think of any thing else to write Now.

With lots of Love and Kisses to all. Don't forget to write often as that is about all I have to look forward to for a while. How is the Kids getting along. Well will close again for sure. With all my love and best wishes.

PVT. Meyers

April-13-44

Dearest Mom-all,

Well will try to scribble a few lines To Night. just got to the Brk's it is 9:00 was on K.P. today since 4:00 A.M. Boy am I tired, got your letter when I got to the Brk's and to top it all off they came over and got us about 2:00 oclock and we each got two More shots, one in each arm. It isn't so sore yet. Well Mom that boy you was talking about is in the same Co. but a different Brks. What is the Matter he don't write and who is the woman. I don't like to fool around with some bodys else Bussines, But you write her and tell her he is O.K. I see him every day. I also got a letter from Howard[17] to day also Lula R.[18] Well Mom we sure have been busy. I haven't had a chance to write for two days and I was beginning to think you had broken your arm or else throwed your pencil away. Well, Mom I think I had better close for to night and get ready to hit the hay. We have to Pack a combat Pack, so I suppose we will take a hike to morrow. Tell Shirley I got her tooth. Well Mom I don't know what to tell you about coming down here, someday if I get a good chance I will go in to Tyler that is the closest Town and see what it is like. Well it is about time for the lights to go out so will close until to morrow Night. Maybe I will have a little More time. I hope so any way. Good-bye and Good wishes with Lots of Love and Kisses to all.

PVT. Meyers

Camp-Fannin-Texas
April-15-1944

Dearest Mom-all,

Well here it is Saturday Night about 9:30 and I am ready to go to bed. Paul and I went to the show to-Night. I wasn't to hot. It was a musical, you know I don't go for them so Much. I got two letters from you today. Mom you don't have to send them air mail if you don't want to. Paul got a letter from his wife to day that was Mailed the same day yours was, so it doesn't Make Much difference how you send them just as long as they come often. I got a letter from Howard, and one from Jett this week besides about 4 or 5 from you and one from Lula.

Well we had it pretty easy today. We had to make up a couple of classes we Missed the other day when we were on K.P. Then we had Inspection at noon. This P.M. we Marched about 3 Miles out in the woods and put up our Tent's then tore them down and rolled them Back up and Marched back to camp. Changed to our dress uniforms and stand Retreat.[19] The fellow that sleeps under Me his Pack came unrolled on the way in. He had to go over to the guard house to Night and roll his Pack 50 times. Say Mom if I have any undershirts that are any good will you send them to Me. If I haven't any you don't Need to get Me any because I can get them here cheaper than you can at home.

We have to change every Night. This sand sure gets into every thing and the wind blows almost all day long. We come in at Night our hair is about as yellow as butter. Well Mom Paul and I are going over to the Service Club to morrow and get our Pictures taken. I guess Next week we are going to start wearing our Summer uniforms I want to get it taken before then. Say I have been wondering wether you had enough Fuel oil or not or did you get any more Stamps.[20] Well Mom I think I will close and go take a shower and go to bed. I will try and write again to-morrow. I don't think I will have to work to-morrow only we have to have our Rifles Inspected at 2:00 P.M. Well will close for Now. With Lots of Love and Kisses to all.

Ans Soon.
P.S. how are all the sick Including yourself?
B-P.VT. Meyers No Stripes Yet

Camp-Fannin-Texas
April-16-1944

Dearest Mom-all,

Well I haven't got Much time until the lights go out but will scribble a few lines. We have been pretty busy all day. At 9:30 A.M. The Air Force from some Near by Base we here and put on a little show. They had a Brass

Band and everything. Boy you should have seen Me strut. We really put on the dog. It lasted about 2 hours. Then we came back and cleaned our Rifles. We had Inspection at 2:00 P.M. We had Turkey again for Dinner and chicken for supper. The turkey was so dam Tough couldn't stick a fork in the gravy. Chicken wasn't Much better. After Inspection Paul and I went over to the P.X. I bought a Carton of Cigarettes $1.30 and a cake of soap. After supper we went to the show. say I almost fergot I washed this Morn. Ha. Ha. I will be a New Man after I get home. Say I heard today that they were going to send everybody with children before Pearl harbor to Indiana or Kentucky to finish our Basic Training. I am ready to go to Night if they say the word. I sure am sick of this place. Well Mom I think I had better sign off and get ready for bed the Cpl. Just told us we are going out to drill all day to-morrow and eat out in the field so I will Need a lot of sleep. I wrote to Jett to Night and have to shave yet. Say My watch quit running all together. I am going to send it home, you take it up to Kohns and see what they will do about it. I think the Main Spring is broken. Say you don't Need to send Me any underwear. If I get transferred closer home I want you to come down and see Me right away. I will let you know later. Well this is all for Now. hoping this finds all feeling better. Ans. Real Soon.
   With all My Love and Kisses,
   B-PVT. Meyers
   P.S. Did you get the Pillow Top

                                        Camp-Fannin
                                        April-17-1944

Dearest Mom-all,
   Well I guess I have a little time before the lights go out, so will try and drop you a few lines. I just got done shaving and taking a shower. Am feeling pretty good Now. one of the boys went over to the P.X. and I sent over and got a pint of Ice Cream. We can get a pint for $.14 It tastes pretty good after being out all day. We left this Morning at 7:15 and didn't get in until 5:00 this eve. They brought our dinner out in the field to us. We got More out thier than we do at the Mess Hall so far it has all been pretty good, but I would rather be home. Paul Spillman is having trouble with his legs. I guess his arches are broken down, he went to the Hospital this Morn, and they taped his legs and feet. Well I got a letter from Etta today, also from you and the Kid's. tell them I really enjoyed it very Much and to write again soon.
   How is all of the sick getting along, tell Elsie I was going to send her a Card, but Couldn't get any. Well it is about time for the lights to go out so will close for to Night answer real soon. With lots of Love and Kisses-
   PVT. Meyers

Camp-Fannin
April-19-1944

Dearest Mom-all,
Well received your letter today that you wrote the 14th also one from My dad. Sure was glad to hear from all of you. How is Elsie getting along by Now? better I hope. I am getting along pretty good now, only it is getting pretty hot. We were out to day. We were down to our under shirts part of the time they had us throwing real hand Grenades we had to wear our steel helmets. Boy are they heavy. I should have a Neck like a Bull when I get home.

I was going to write last Night but we had to go on a scouting tour didn't get back until 10:00. They had a big can of coffee made for us when we got back. It tasted pretty good. I got a letter from Bus yesterday Noon. I answered it yesterday Noon.

Well how is the weather up that way? Right Now it is raining and hailing here. Paul and I were over to the P.X. a little bit. I got you another Pillow Top. I will Mail it to night. It isn't like the other. I think it is prettier. You can let me know what you think. I suppose you will disagree as usual HA HA. I also got Me two under shirts. We can get stuff like that we Need at almost cost. It is Goverment operated. Candy Bars .04 each, Ice Cream $.14 Pint, My under shirts were only $.33 each they look pretty good to. Well Mom I think I better close and write to dad, also owe Etta a letter also Lula R. I don't know wether I will catch up or Not Maybe I will some of these days. If I don't get to busy and they are keeping us pretty busy Most of the time. Well this is all for tonight, answer real soon as I look for a letter every day. I will write every day If I have time. Must close and Shave and take a shower. With lots of Love and Kisses.

PV.T. Meyers
Tell the Kids I sail hello. Say I got a Card from That Kantner Boys Mother, so I suppose I will have to answer.
XXXXX

Camp-Fannin
April-20-1944

Dear Mom-all,
Well another day is about done. I have got all My work done for tonight and am ready for bed. In fact am in bed. Wish I was home. We had a pretty hard day today. and boy was it hot about 90° in the shade, and no shade. We had to dig a Fox hole and then get in it and they run over us with an old tank thier was about 20 of us that they didn't have time to run over, but I don't

care. We have about 8 hours of training each day. It wouldn't be so bad if they wouldn't Make us go so dam fast. that is what gets us, but I suppose we will get used to it. They have the word going around that we will finish our training here in 12 weeks. If we do I will be home about the time school is out. If it is 17 weeks it will be about the first of August.

About coming down I don't know when I will get to town. We don't get a chance to go through the week and on Sunday we have so Much work to do of our own it is to dam late, but maybe I will get to town soon.

How is all the folks getting along by Now. I got a letter from dad yesterday. don't know when I will get it answered, but will try Sat. Night or Sunday. Well it is about time for the lights to go out so had better close for tonight. Tell Elsie while she is laying around taking life easy to drop Me a line, and I will try and ans, sure am glad to hear from any body, even (Mary) Ha. Ha. haven't yet, Belive Me. Well Good Night and good Luck, with lots of Love and Kisses to all.

Tell the Kids I said Hello,
B-PVT. Meyers

Camp-Fannin-Texas
April-23-1944

Dearest-Mom-all,

Well as I haven't got anything to do this afternoon, I will try and catch up on My writing a little bit. I just wrote to dad and want to write to Etta and Walter Kah yet. Was going to write some this A.M. but just got My washing done and they took a bunch of us out to put up some targets to practice with our Rifles and Machine guns. After dinner which wasn't to hot Paul and I went over to the service Mens Club to get our pictures taken, but couldn't get in. So we came back and went to the show. It was pretty good. Andy Hardy in (Blonde Trouble) I think I will spend the rest of the day and evening writing letters.

Well Mom I don't think you will get down to Texas to see Me as all the talk here is that our Basic will be finished in 12 weeks. Then we get a Furlough and will be assigned to some training camp to replace younger Men for overseas Duty. I don't care if they ship Me yet tonight. I am getting pretty dam tired of this sand and wind. half the time your eyes are so full you can't see. the other half thier isn't any thing to see but sand.

Well how are you getting along financially and otherwise? And did you get the fuel oil straightened out? I hope so because I suppose you Need fire quite abit of the time yet we don't Need Much here once in awhile in the Morning we turn the heater on. It only takes about five Minutes for it to heat up. Does Steve know yet when he will have to go? Did Gordon Walters[21] ever leave? I don't suppose so. I guess I didn't Suck Duncan's Ass enough.

But we will get along and after it is over we won't have to be ashamed to look them all in the face.

How is Sallie and Elsie getting along? You Never did say what was the Matter with her, or is it a Military Secret. Ha. Ha. Our Company Commander is being sent to another Camp. they took up a collection for him the other day, and got him a wrist watch $137.50 boy was it a honey. Say don't tell any one about this, as we are Not supposed to do it. I haven't sent My watch yet. I will try and send it some day next week. We have to go to Regemential Post office to Mail anything like that. Did you get the other Pillow Top I sent you? Say are those shoes Carroll[22] gave Me any good at all. If you think I could wear them around here a little at evening and on Sunday you can send them to Me also some under shirts if they are any good. and if I have any handkerchiefs. don't send them registered or I will have to go to the Post office to get it.

How does your dad like his Job? is he still running the show. Well I think I had better sign off and write to Etta I got a letter to day from Myrtle, Sam and Margaurite.[23] Good bye and Good Luck with lots of Love and Kisses. ans. often

PVT. Meyers

Camp-Fannin
April-24-44

Dearest Mom-all,

Well got all the work done for tonight so will try and answer your letter. I don't get done this early very often. Usually write and then shave and take a shower. I should of went and got another G.I. haircut tonight but am going to wait until the Middle of the week. We are supposed to get one every week. I didn't get it cut last week. I suppose the Sargent will eat My ass out about it one of these day, but we are getting used to that. I have been pretty lucky so far they haven't said Much to Me. A good Soldier Ha. Ha.

We started in on our Rifle practice to day just aiming. I guess we will have that Most of the week, then Next week we go out on the range for the real stuff.

I got a letter from Bus today. The way he writes he sure is homesick. I want to write to him tonight. Tell Elsie I got her letter to day and will try to answer it soon. I am about out of Stationery. I sent over to the P.X. with one of the boys to get some.

Say you ought to see us in Bayonet practice. They have a loud Speaker and one of the Lietunents gives the orders. They have us lay on our bellies, over on our backs, up on our feet and double time, lay on our back and go through the Motion of riding a bycycle. Boy if it don't Kill you it will Make a dam good Man out of you. Tell Steve it would really take his Bellie off. and they have an obstacle course that really is a honey. You start out jumping a hurdle about 2 ½ feet high, then you jump a ditch about 6 feet wide, over a wall about 7 feet high under some bars about 1 ½ feet off the ground, climb a rope about 20 feet high, and Most every thing but stand on your head. I suppose they will have us doing that before long. Well Mom how are you all getting along. I am getting along as good as could be expected am feeling pretty good. Got weighed Sunday. 182 ½ have gained a little. So far haven't Missed a Meal. Paul isn't getting along so good, he has Missed 3 or 4 days so far, if he Misses Many More he will have to fall back into another cycle to finish his Basic.[24] Well I think I better close and write to Bus before the lights go out. have you heard anything from Killian[25] I wrote to him a couple of weeks ago, but haven't received an answer yet. If you think about some evening call up Ruth and ask her if he has been Moved. You call for Haspel's on east Pearl Street. Well good Night with Lots of Love and Kisses to all. ans Soon.

PVT. Carl Meyers

Camp-Fannin
April-25-1944

Dear Mom-all,

Just a line this evening to let you know I am still alive and kicking. Although I am pretty tired. We are still on Rifle drilling it is pretty tough and that Bayonet practice is really tough. We also had to run the obstacle course. I don't know wether I will be able to get out of bed in the Morning or Not.

Well how is everybody getting along at Lima? Fine I hope. How is dad getting along. haven't heard from any of them for several day's. I wrote to almost all of them sunday, so had ought to get a lot of Mail about the last of the week. Didn't get any at all today, hope will do better to morrow. It really helps to keep a fellows spirit up to get a little Mail each day.

Well Mom I think I will be home about the time you are expecting to come down here. They are talking a lot about this 12 weeks basic. That would sure suit Me fine. I would like to see everybody back home real soon. Has Steve heard anything when he will have to go? I don't think they are going to take very Many More Married Men unless it is for limited service. I don't know what they will do with them. I don't think Paul is going to be able to take this training. Well Mom I have got to write to Bus So I guess I better sign off for tonight. With Lots of Love and Kisses. As ever, yours.

B-PVT. Meyers

Camp-Fannin
April-27-1944

Dearest-Mom-all,

Well received your letter this evening. Had begun to think you had broken your arm or something. Also got a letter from Margaurite. haven't got Much to do this evening. It is only 7:30 and am all done but taking a shower and shaving. That wont take very long. Will do that about 9:00. Say the Company Commander Made a little speech to day about having our wives or anybody coming down here to visit us. he said it was almost impossible to get any place to stay and that from Now on we couldn't tell from one day until the Next whether we could get to town in the evening. I still think I will be home before then. We are spending about all of our time with Rifle practice. Next week we go out on the Range and start to fire real ammunition. They are sure giving us plenty of training on how to shoot. Tell Steve when I get home he Might as well hang up his gun and carry My game. They are learning us to shoot from five different positions. Boy are some of them hard to get into. The different positions are laying down, sitting, kneeling, Squatting and Standing. We have to stand erect and then get in these different positions. Shoot one shot put in a full clip and shoot 8 More times in 51 seconds. that is pretty fast for an old Man don't you think so? The Rifle is semi automatic shoots 8 time's with one clip.

Well Mom I will try my best to get that picture taken Sunday. If I am not on Detail of some kind. We have changed to our summer uniforms this week. I don't like the shirts, the collars don't look Neat. Well Mom I think I better close and write to Walter Kah to Night. I promised him I would and haven't done so yet. Also to Myrtles family I have gotten two letters from them and haven't answered either as yet. I don't suppose I will get to write to Morrow Night as we have to get ready for Inspection Saturday Morning. Will close with load's of Love and Kisses to all.

As ever your Sweet Pappy,
PVT. Meyers

Camp-Fannin
April-29-1944

Dear Mom-

Well as I have a little time before lights go out will scribble a few lines. Received your letter today also one from My dad and one from Lula R. sure glad to get them. Well how is the weather up in Ohio? It sure is wet as hell here right Now it rained from about 4:00 P.M. until 8:00. We had to March about two Miles in the rain. We had our rain coats on but our shoes were soaked and our legs from our knees down.

Paul and I went to the show about 8:00 just got back and got shaved. the lights don't go out until 10:45 on Saturday Nite.

Well we go on the range Next week to start firing real ammunition. I don't know if I will be able to hit any thing or Not. I do know I have a lot of washing to do in the Morning. I think I will get up early in the Morning and do it before chow. Paul and I May go into town to Morrow. I also want to get that Picture taken. They took a picture of the whole Company last evening. I will send you one as soon as we get them. Good-Night and Best of Luck and Kisses.

PVT. Meyers

Camp-Fannin
April-30-1944

Dearest-Mom,

Well just a line to let you know I received the box to day, and the shoes are to small. I think that I will sell them to somebody and send you the Money for another pair. They were long enough but to Narrow. Do you have any More stamps? The fellow that wants to buy them is an Indian and I don't think he has any stamps. Couldn't you get a shoe the same last as My black ones. They sure felt good. You don't Need to be in a hurry to get them. If I don't sell them in a couple of days we will send them back. How is the weather at home Now? It sure is raining like hell here has been since about 5:00 P.M.

Well to Morrow we go out to start firing the real lead. We have two weeks of Rifle practice-and then two weeks of Machine gun practice. After that we have 60.M.M. Mortar and heavy weapon's. Say has thier been anything in the paper about us old devils getting a discharge? some fellow here said it came over the Radio that all of us over 26 would be. Boy I sure hope so. I Could really enjoy Myself for about a week. Tell your Dad to have a good supply of Beer on hand Because I am really going to take a lot of it if I ever get home, and I hope it won't be to long. Well Mom I got My picture taken today. You can put it in the Parlor or on the back Porch which ever you like. I don't suppose you have room on the Back porch, Ha Ha. They wasn't very good. That Cap shaded My forehead. I wish I had taken it with My own Cap on Now. If I ever get to town I am going to have a big one taken. I just showed those pictures to one of the boys, he said for Me Not to send them home. When you look at them I suppose you will faint but I am Not this bad off. I will send you some better ones soon. Well Mom I think I had better close and get ready to turn in we have to get up at 4:45 while we are on the range. Say did you ever get My Razor back. I can use it down here. If you let Me know how Much it costs I will send you the Money. I almost fergot.

Monday is Pay Day the first for some time. Well good Night and hoping to hear from you real soon with Lots of love and Kisses.

PVT. Meyers

P.S. Am sending the Kids some Post Cards.

Later No Stamps

Wed. Morn

Dear Mom,

Just a line this Morn have got about 5 Min until chow. We don't get done until 11:00 P.M. at Night am doing O.K. so far have been Shooting in the grade of a Sharp shooter. How is all? O.K. I hope Maybe will find time this eve to write More with Love to all and Kisses.

PVT. MEYERS

Camp-Fannin
May-3-1944

Dear Mom-all,

Just a line to Night to let you know I am still partly alive anyway. We sure have been putting in long days. Get up at 4:45 and usually don't get to bed until about 11:00.

We leave Camp at 6:00. March about two Miles, and fire until about 7:00 P.M. Until we get in and get chow and clean our Rifles and Shave and take a bath it is about 11:00 sometimes later. I have been doing pretty good, Shot in the expert class to day on the 300 yard Range, Rapid fire. That is 9 shots in 51 seconds. I got 40 Points of a Possible 45. Which isn't bad for a small town hick. This afternoon I was on pit detail. I was the guard: Sit on my ass all afternoon. I was going to write a letter, but didn't have any Paper. This is the first chance I have had to write since sunday. got a letter from Bus and one from Betty[26] yesterday and one from Lula today. Bus also sent me his picture. Say what do you think of My pictures. They sure were rotten don't you think. I am going to have some more taken only am going to wear My overseas cap. The one I had on before belonged at the place I had it taken and it shaded My forehead, looked like your Neighbors. Ha. Ha. Well we got our first pay Monday. Boy was it a big one $20.50 Not quite as much as I used to draw. Have you got your check for May yet. Well Mom it is about time for the lights to go out so better close and get ready to hit the hay. It won't be long until time to get up, hoping to hear from you real soon. With lots of Love and Kisses to all.

as ever

PVT. Meyers

Camp-Fannin
May-4-1944

Dear Mom-all,

Well just a line this eve to let you know I am still alive and O.K. since we have been on the range They don't drill us so hard but we put in a lot of hours.

We were on the 500 yard range to day. I shoot 35 out of a possible 40 the first time this afternoon we shot for record I didn't do quite so good, only got 33 out of 40, but for 500 yard that is in the expert class. To Morrow we fire for record on the 200 and 300 yard range from about 4 or 5 Positions. I think I can qualify pretty good so far all totaled I have qualified as a sharp shooter. I think I can do better from Now on. I had a lot of trouble with My Rifle, but have got it fixed Now I think. Had it to the repair shop three times.

Well how is everybody getting along back home? Fine I hope. Tell Buck[27] he is a better looking soldier then his Dad. How do you like My pictures? I think I will go into Tyler sunday and have My picture taken again. I hope it is better then the others. If I go I will send those shoes and My watch back. When you get the watch take it up to Kohns and tell them when I got it and see if they won't Make it right. I think they should. If they don't just put it in the safety Deposit box till I get home, as I don't need it out here. They tell us when to go and come back and this sand goes right through a watch. About half the watches out Don't run right. They don't read time like we do in civilian time. They don't stop at 12:00 Noon. One oclock in the P.M. they call 1300 and right on up to 2400 then start over. But it still don't Make the days a dam bit shorter. Well Mom I think I had better close and write to Bus. I also have to write to P.S. Killian received a letter from him the other day. He is still in the Hospital but getting along O.K. Tell Shirley I will be looking for a picture of her and one of you also soon. Well good-Night and good luck to all. Must get some sleep so I can see to Shoot to-Morrow. With Lots of Love and Kisses,

   as ever
   S. S. PVT. Meyers
   h h
   a o
   r o
   p t
      e
      r

Chapter 2

Camp-Fannin
May-6-1944

Dear Mom-all,

Just a line this evening while I am waiting on Paul to shave. Then we are going to the show. I suppose you are getting ready to go get drunk. Well we finished up shooting to day for our record firing with the M.1. Rifle. I qualified as a Sharp Shooter. Thier was only 14 out of 50. one expert, so I guess I will get a Medal of some kind. I didn't do so hot in record firing as I did in practice.

Has Steve heard anything when he has to go? And how is Toot's getting along? Is she up and around yet? I hope she is getting along O.K.

Well I don't know what we will be doing Next week. But I don't think we will put in as Many hours as we did this week. Maybe I will get to write a little More then I have been. I think Paul and I will go to town to Morrow. If we do I am going to have My picture taken again.

Say I sold those shoes to Shorty Pyles. I will send you the Money when I write to Morrow he said he would get them to Night. Well I will close Now until tomorrow. With Lots of Love and Kisses,

S.S. PVT Carl Meyers

Camp-Fannin
May-7-1944

Dear Mom-all,

Well just a line this evening to let you know I am still alive. Paul, Shorty that Kantner boy and I went into Tyler this P.M. We had a lot of fun and also some pictures taken. I sent them from town. If you don't like them you can burn them. I think it is a little better then the others. I also sent the kids each a little present. They will all come together. I forgot about the pictures and addressed them all to the kids so you can claim the pictures. I also sent the Company picture we had taken the other day.

Well Mom Paul and I just got back from the show it was pretty good. We went last Night but it wasn't so good. You ask about My furlough, we don't seem to hear Much about it any More but I do think we will finish our training in about 12 or 14 weeks. Thier is a fellow here from Lima that is a Buck Sargent who makes up the training schedule he was home on a furlough and say My address in the paper. When he came back he came over and looked Me up. We had quite a chat his Name is Baker. He lives at 764 West Market. I think that is the Number am not sure. If I get to see him again I am going to try to find out for sure about our training. He seems like a pretty good fellow.

Well how is everybody getting along anyway? Have you got your check yet? Paul said his wife got hers about the third of May, so you should have gotten yours by Now. Paul and Shorty and I got on the wrong Bus coming home it took us one hour and half to get back to camp and only about 7 or 8 Miles but we had a lot of fun. But I think the Next time I head for town it will be Lima Ohio. I don't seem to get any kicks out of going to a strange town like that you have to be careful. They have M.P. and Courtesy Officers all over town. If you meet a commissioned officer and don't Salute him they take your Name and turn it in to company Headquarters and then put you on the carpet, and Make you work like hell some Nights for a couple of hours.

Say Mom I sold those shoes for $5.00 am sending the Money if you have an extra stamp you can get Me another pair or else take My black ones and get them dyed. If you get New ones get them pretty wide like My black ones. Well Mom this is about all I can think of to write this evening. So think I had better sign off for Now hoping to hear from you real soon. With lots of Love and kisses to all.

S.S. PVT. Carl Meyers

Boy wait till I get that Medal. I sure will have a job sewing Buttons on My Shirt (Ha. Ha.)

(Good Night to all)

Camp-Fannin
May-8-1944

Dear Mom-all,

just a line this evening to let you know that I am very unhappy. They just put a Notice on the Bulletin Board that all of our Platoon is on K.P. tomorrow. Have to get up at 4:00 A.M. in the Morning. It is about as bad as the extra board for the Bus Company, only I do wish it was. I think when this is over we will Move on a farm and do as we Dam please and I hope it won't be long. I don't think it will be. They read the latest News each day direct from the War Department and they sure are raising Hell over thier. It can't end to soon to suit Me.

Well how is everybody getting along? Fine I hope. I am getting along pretty good. Only lost about four pounds today, one of these Sargents ate it off My ass. Boy they sure enjoy getting on somebody. They have to chew on somebody every day or they don't feel good. But it don't hurt after it is over. We kid each other about it so it is all in the days work. This was My first and the other boys really got a kick out of it. Well Mom I think it is about time to sign off and get ready for bed. 4:00 A.M. will roll around pretty quick in the Morning. Say I almost forgot Did you get the stuff I Sent you and the Kids. I also sent $5.00 I got for the shoes. let me know as soon as you get them. Well Good Night and Good Luck to all with Lots of Love and Kisses to all. as ever

S. S. PVT. Meyers
h h
a o
r o
p t
  e
  r

P.S. So far have only lost one Button and haven't even got My Medal yet. Ha. Ha.

Camp-Fannin
May-10-1944

Dear Mom-all,

Well as I have all the work done for another day will try to drop you a few lines to let you know that I am alive and still kicking although it don't seem to do Me any good. How is the weather up in Ohio? beginning to warm up a little I suppose. It is getting pretty warm here have been running around all evening with just My pants and shoes on. I suppose it will be plenty hot in a few days.

Well I survived K.P. again. But that is about all. We didn't get done until about 9:00 P.M. One company was out on the range and didn't get in until about 7:30. Then we had to clean up after that. Boy I am getting to be a expert (house keeper) Ha. Ha. Our squad has the job of cleaning the Hut every Morning this week. Thier is three squads so we get it every three weeks. It isn't so bad if they all pitch in and help, But thier is always a couple that try to get out of it. We call them Gold Bricks in the army. Well when do you think you are coming down if you come. I don't know what to tell you to do if you do get to come. But if the rest of the women come it won't be so bad. How are they coming? On the train or Drive? I just don't know for sure when we will go on Bivouac.[28] But when we do it will be for two weeks and during that time we will be out of camp all the time. That is almost at the end of our Basic Training. Well Mom it is awful lonesome here without you. But it isn't so bad as if thier wasn't any one here that I didn't know. and it also seems like the time goes awful fast. I guess that is because we are so busy.

Say did you get the pictures and things I sent the kids, also the $5.00 I sent for the shoes. You don't need to get Me anymore. If you could just get those Black ones Dyed. They would do until later. Well Mommy I think I

had better close and write to Margaurite. I have received Two letters from her and haven't answered either one. So don't forget to write whenever you can and I will do the same. With all My Love and Kisses to all. as ever,
PVT. Meyers

Camp-Fannin
May-11-1944

Dear Mom-all,

Well just a line before the lights go out to let you know I am still alive. Don't know if I will be after tomorrow or Not. We are going out about 8 Miles in the Morning, Stay all day and eat C. Rations[29] for Dinner and Supper. They gave them to us tonight four little cans. I don't know if I can live on that or Not. If you don't hear from Me for a while you will know I Starved to Death. Ha. Ha. But I suppose I can stand it. Several before Me have and I guess all of them across the pond are eating them.

Well have any you got your check yet? I hope so. We get paid the last day of each Month. I don't know what I will get this Month. I don't think it will be Much different. I hope it isn't Much less anyway. Well we are taking up Machine Guns Now. We were over in a big Hall this P.M. and shooting them loaded with Marbles of some kind and Shoot by air pressure at air planes. Tell Dick he should have been here. He probably could have done better then any of us. Well Mom it is about time for the lights to go out so I think I had better close and get ready for Bed hoping to hear from you real soon.

With Lots of Love and Kisses to all,
PVT. Meyers

Camp-Fannin
May-12-1944

Dear Mom-all,

Just a line to Night and it won't be very long. It is almost time for the lights to go out. I just got done shaving and taking a shower. We didn't get in until late and it was about 6 or 7 Miles out to the Range when we started back. They were on the Force March. It is awful fast. We take 120 Steps a Minute. If [you] think that isn't fast the Next time you go down to the Store just try it. I think thier was about 20 Men fell out the first Mile. Then one of the officers Made them Slow down and Boy was it hot. Our clothes was ringing wet with Sweat when we got in. We also had field Rations out on the Range at Noon. It was hash in one can about 2/3 the size of a can of Milk, the other can had a drink of some kind they have Several different kinds Mine was Lemon extract for Lemonade. Also Sugar 3 cigarettes, Some candy, and crackers, and were they hard. But it seemed to fill up pretty good. We were also supposed to eat the same for supper. I haven't ate Mine yet and don't think I will. I ate a pint of Ice Cream and Drank about a barrell of water. I guess Paul passed clear out coming in tonight. But I saw him a while ago. He was feeling pretty good then. Say you have heard about the Yellow Rose of Texas. Out where we were to day I Marched through a field of about 20 or 25 acres of Nothing but Roses. All colors and Sizes. I grabbed one am going to tear it up and put it in the letter. If I could would send you a whole box but they wouldn't be any good. Say haven't you got those last pictures I sent you. I was hoping you would get them before Sunday. Well Mom I think I had better Sign off for to Night. It is about time for the lights to go out. With Lots of Love and Kisses to all.

as ever

PVT. Meyers

P.S. Say I forgot to tell you I got a letter from Kelley, the cashier up at the garage.

Good-Night

Camp-Fannin
May-14-1944

Dear Mom-all,

Well here it is Sunday again and Mothers Day. I sure would like to be home with you or at least have been able to send you some flowers. But you can't do a dam thing here that we would like to. It seems about the time we think we are going to have a spare Minute they find something for us to do. Paul and I went to the show last Night. I did My washing after we came back. Then this Morning I had to clean My rifle and wash My Leggings and Shoes. It sure Rained here yesterday P.M. for about half hour and did we get soaked. Didn't even have our Rain Coats with us. I don't know what I will do this P.M. go to the show I suppose. I do know I hain't going to hang around the Hut. That is where you get a lot of work.

Say did you get the stuff I sent home. Thier was a picture of Me and one of Shorty-Paul-that Kantner Boy and Myself. A pin for each of the Kid's and a picture of the company. When you get that look at the fellow on each end on the bottom Row. And see if they look like Twins. They aren't. It is the same fellow. They took it with a Moving Picture Camera as soon as they took the left end he ran around and got on the other end. He sure is a ornery Cuss. I don't know if you can see the Stripes on his sleeve or Not. He is a corpal and a Nice fellow.

I was going to have My picture taken again to day but we were out on the range yesterday and we had to fire left handed laying flat on the ground. My Rifle kicked Me twice and I have a Nice cut just below My left eye and also kind of black. I hit both targets so I don't Mind so Much. got a pretty good score for all My pains. Say Mom will you go up town and get Me a couple of those things to hold a collar down. I had one and a fellow wanted it pretty bad he offered Me $.50 for it and I sold it. So if you send Me Some I will send you the Money C.O.D. Ha. Ha.

Say did you get your check? If you haven't and thier is anything I can do be sure and let Me know. And if you Need the Money cash in the rest of those Bonds. I think we are doing our part anyway. Got a letter from Gett[30] yesterday. I guess they are having a hell of a time with the Drivers. I think that I will write to Duncan to day. Maybe he can get Me out of this dam place. I see in the paper they aren't going to take anymore of us old Men. Ha. Ha. And I also think we will be released as soon as our training is over and the way they are rushing it I don't think it will be to long. I sure hope Not anyway.

Well Mom as I can't think of anymore gossip right Now I think I had better close and write to some body else a while. I got to write to Gett-Kelley-and Howard until Noon as Paul and I are going to the Show this P.M. If I think of anything else I will write again this eve. With all My Love and Kisses to all. I remain the same,
PVT. Carl Meyers

Camp-Fannin
May-16-1944

Dear Mom-all,

Just a line between jumps to let you know we sure are on the go. last Night I was on guard Duty only had to walk guard two hours but we had to go to guard School from 7:30 P.M. until 10:00. Then I went on Duty until 12:00. But we had to stay at the guard house until 6:00 A.M. All we had to sleep on was an army cot like we have at home. I am about all in this evening. And we aren't done yet. This A.M. we were out on the Range firing the Carbine. I qualified as (SHARP SHOOTER). Ask Steve if that is right. Ha. Ha. got 125 out of 150. It is the same Caliber as our other Rifle only it is a lot Shorter. Tomorrow we start out at 7:30 A.M. until 5:00 P.M. Then we are off until about 8:00. Then we go out on some kind of a Night Problem.[31] I don't know what it is for sure we have got to go to some kind of a show yet this evening. Then we have to clean our Rifles. I don't know what time we will get done. But I do know I am ready to go to bed as soon as possible. It sure is going to be a long day ahead and one behind.

Well Mom I got My shoes and chewing gum last evening. I haven't had time to try them on very good. I sure hope I can wear them. They sure are Nice. Tell Elsie I said Thanks for the Flowers. You should be here and see our Roses. did you get the one I sent you and have you received the stuff I sent you and the kids. Well Mom it is about time for the show so will finish later. Well the show is over and I am all ready to hit the hay just got done

Shaving and taking a shower. Say you don't need to send My Razar for a while. It is getting pretty hot here and I don't think this sand would be very good for it and I couldn't use it out on Bivouac. I got a letter from O.E. Monsa today. I guess he is getting better but Slow. Well Mom I think I had better close for to Night will try to drop you a few lines to Morrow evening before we take off.

With lots of love and Kisses to all,
as ever PVT. Meyers

Camp-Fannin
May-17-1944

Dear Mom-All,

Will try to scribble a few lines this evening before we go out, and Maybe can write a few More in the Morning. I don't know for sure just what we are going to do out to Night, leaving camp at 8:00 P.M. get back at 11:00. It is going to be along day and a short Night, but I just looked at the scheudle for to Morrow and it don't look so hard. We have a parade of some kind to Morrow evening, and we are going to practice a couple of hours for that. We also have to go out on the Bivouac area some place and set up our tents.

I got the letter Elsie wrote this evening. I thought at first it was a anouncement of a (Birth) In that big envelope, Ha. Ha. Say did you get that picture of the Company? Well Mom it is about time to go so will try to write a little More in the Morning.

Well Mom here it is another day we got in at 11:30: P.M. Last Night. They let us sleep an hour later this Morning. All we did last Night was March out a couple Miles and sit in the Stands. While They fired off different kinds of Shells, it wasn't so bad after all. Say the Company Commander told us yesterday That our training was half over. So Maybe we will be home soon. Well Mom Must close for Now More Later. With Lots of Love and Kisses to all, as ever,
PVT. Meyers

Camp-Fannin
May-17-1944

Dear Mom-all,

Well just a line to let you know I am still alive. Though almost smothered to death. It sure is hot. We were out on a long March today. It was about 6 Miles each way with our full field pack which weights about 60 pounds, but all we did when we got out thier was set up our tents, eat dinner, pack up and come back in. We set around in the shade for about two hours. Then we had a big parade this eve they gave the Medal to the highest score for shooting in the Battalion, a kid in our company got it. 194 points out of a possible 210. It sure was a Nice Statue, and then we Marched around the Drill field awhile all decked out in our Kakhies with Rifles, Belts, and Bayonets on the Rifle, and they had a Military band playing. Boy you should have seen us Strut. I don't know what the Major thought of it. All the big Shits was out. We got in from our March at 3:00. We had until 5:00 to clean our Rifles and shave and take a shower and get ready for the parade. After chow I had to do some washing and get ready for Inspection in the Morning.

Well Mom I don't know if I am going to be able to wear these shoes or Not. I have got them on Now but they are pretty tight. I haven't walked on them so if they are to tight I can send them back. Well Mom it is about time to hit the hay and I have got to shine My shoes yet so will sign off for Now. With lots of love and Kisses to all. as ever

PVT. Meyers

Camp-Fannin
May-19-1944

Dear Mom-all,

Well we got the Hut all Sweep and scrubbed, ready for Inspection in the Morn. We had Rifle and Personal Inspection to day. Passed O.K. it won't hurt Me any to Morrow. It is just the Battalion Inspection. Well how is the weather in Ohio? We had a Nice Shower here to day. It cooled things off pretty good. It is going to be a good Night to sleep. Say did you have enough fuel oil with the extra you got? Have you taken the storie down yet? I don't Suppose you will have room on the back Porch for it. Ha. Ha. Say Mom Don't spend all that Money unless you have to because I don't think I will have enough to come home on when I get My Furlough, but you can cash in those Bond's any time you want to, and I want you to If you Need it. Say thier is a guy here in this Hut That is a cousin to Ruth Killian.[32] His Name is Harold Haspel. If you see Ruth ask her about him. His home is at Dayton Ohio, also a fellow that knows Sam's brother at Tipp City. I forget his Name. Well Mom just had some Ice Cream and cake. We sent over to the P.X. and one of the boys got a cake from home so we had the works. Well I think I had better sign off and write to Kah, and I have to shave and take a shower yet. With lots of Love and Kisses to all, as ever,

PVT. Meyers

P.S. Say I think I will go to town Sunday and Mail those Shoes home. you can take them back and get your Money back and I will wait until I get home to get some.

Camp-Fannin
May-21-1944

Dear Mom-all,

Well another week is past and it is Sunday. I wish this was the last week. But it isn't. So I guess thier isn't anything we can do about it. I have been pretty busy all day. Saturday P.M. we were out on the Range all day, and did it ever rain. We were pretty well soaked when we got in and it took us quite a while to clean our Rifles and oil them and Paul and I went to the Show got back about 10:00. Then we washed for about an hour. Then got up this Morn and did some More. I guess I have it all done Now for a couple of days. I sure will be glad when this dam thing is over and I can go home and live like other people. I really don't think it will last very long.

Say Mom I sent those shoes and My watch to town with a fellow, and he Mailed them for Me. Be careful because the watch is in with the shoes. Well how did you like the pictures? I think they are a little better than the first. I don't Suppose that Steve will have to go Now that they have lowered the age limit. I sure hope he doesn't. Well Mom it seems like I can't think of anything Much to write to Night. Paul and I went to the show this P.M. It was real good. Gary Cooper in Doctor Wassell. You ask about Red Herndon he is in another Company. I don't know why they put him in a different Co. he is still in the same Battilion. I see him about every day or so. Well Mom I am getting tired of writing I think I have written about 4 or 5 letters to day. Will try to do better the Next time. With Lots of Love and Kisses to all,

PVT. Carl Meyers

Camp-Fannin
May-22-1944

Dear Mom-all,

Well How is all at home by Now? Fine I hope. I am as good as could be expected. Was on sick call this Morning, got a little Poison Ivey. It took Me all afternoon to get a little box of salve. But I was kind of glad because it sure rained for a bout two hours, and when the rest came in they were soaked to the skin. We have had it pretty easy this evening so far. But you are Never sure we are done until we get to bed. I have got My Rifle cleaned and oiled and it is only 7:15 have got to Shave and take a Shower but it won't take long. Have you got the Hot Water tank hooked up yet? It will soon be hot and then it will be all hot. It is down here. The More we drink the More we want. The only place we get a cold drink is at Chow time. Then it is like a bunch of hogs, all want to drink at once. Well you should have the Shoes and My watch back by the time you get this. If they won't fix My watch free you don't Need to get it fixed as I don't Need it very bad, and everybody seems to have trouble with thiers down here.

Well Mom I don't know what to tell you about when I will be home for sure. They tell us one thing one day and another the Next, but I do know we will get at least 10 days at home when we finish our Basic Training. I really believe that they are going to put us on reserve or something like that when we finish our Basic. I know that I don't want to come back to this place. I would rather go across. It seems the are sending a lot of fellows from here to Indiana and Kentucky for special assignment as M.P. or something.

Say that envelope you sent had Carl Seaman's[33] address on so I guess I will drop them a line. I wrote about all day yesterday, I think about 6 or 7 letters. It seems like home is all I get to write through the week then on Sunday we have to write to all the rest of the Family. Well Mom I think I had better sign off for Now. With Lots of Love and Kisses to all. I remain the same Sweet Daddy, Ha. Ha.

PVT. Meyers

Camp-Fannin
May-23-1944

Dear Mom-all,

Well we just got done this evening and it is about 9:30 so this will probaly be pretty Short. I heard last Night that they are shipping the Pre Pearl Harbor fathers out after 10 weeks training. In fact one company shipped to day to a place in Kentucky.

Wednesday eve

Well Mom didn't have time to finish this last Night. So will try it again. It sure is hot here-and we were on another force March this P.M. four Miles in 50 Minutes I think My Shoes were full of Sweat when we got back. I guess we will have a couple of them every week. But I don't think we will be here very long. I heard this evening that No Pre Pearl Harbor fathers were to be shipped over seas, and all that didn't go over would finish thier Basic in Ten weeks, Then be shipped to Camp Beckenridge Kentucky for some kind of training. I am ready to go any time and if we are only here Ten weeks it won't be long. This is our eighth week here just in case you have lost count. If we go to Ky. I want you to come down as soon as you can. How is Shirley after her Bath? I hope she didn't catch cold. Have you got the Shoes and watch yet? And how did you Make out with them? How is Steve making out with the Navy? Or has he heard any More? I sure hope he doesn't have to go. Is Elsie working yet? Say I got the Tie things to day. Thanks a lot. These dam Shirts we wear The collars just won't lay down. Is Charles School out yet? And how is he getting along? Is he going down to Lulas after school is out? How is your dad getting along? Is he still Selling Beer? Tell him to keep a

good supply on hand for when I come home, because I am getting awful dry. I have only drank one Beer since I been here. Don't you think I am awful good. Well Mom I had better sign off for to Night it is about time for the lights to go out and I have got to take a Shower yet. With Lots of Love and Kisses to all,
    PVT. Meyers

                              Camp-Fannin
                              May-25-1944

Dear Mom-all,

Well just a few lines this evening to let you know I am still among the living though I don't know if I will be tomorrow night or not. We have got some kind of a drill that we are going to wade through a creek, and if it is over my head you know I will just be a drowned Goose Ha Ha. Say haven't you got those shoes and watch yet. Be sure and let me know as soon as you get them. I had the box Insured for $40.

Well how are you getting along with the house cleaning? If all the fellows in this Hut were thier we could clean it up in about 30 minutes. You should see us clean up this joint. If you dont hear from me tomorrow night think nothing of it, for it is clean up night and thier is about 18 of the fellows on guard duty so thier wont be very many to clean up.

How is Shirley getting along after her bath? O.K. I hope. Well Mom I think I had better close and shave. I dont think I will take a shower as I expect to get one tomorrow. Ha Ha. Good night and lots of Love and Kisses to all,
    PVT. Meyers

                              Camp-Fannin
                              May-27-44

Dear Mom-all,

Just a line this evening let you know I am still among the living. Didn't get to write last night. We didn't get the work done until about 10:30 and got in bed about 11:00. We had a pretty tough inspection this A.M. got by O.K. but thier was a lot that didn't they had to clean all the company guns tonight. I have got about all of my washing done for tomorrow, all I have to do is polish my mess kit and wash my leggings. That wont take very long. If they dont catch up with me before noon I am going to take it pretty easy. Paul and I just got back from the show, it wasn't so hot. Dont know what we will do Sunday. May go to church to keep out of work.

Well how is everything going around home? Fine I hope. Say do you have Busses new address? I got a letter from him and Betty last week but I didn't get to answer it yet. So I guess his address is different now. Maybe I will write to him tomorrow.

I suppose he will get it some time. Well Mom I don't know when we will get out of here. They haven't said much the last couple of days but I really don't think it will be very long. I sure hope it isn't. Well Mom will close for tonight, and write more tomorrow. With lots of Love and Kisses. As ever

PVT. Meyers

Camp-Fannin
May-28-1944

Dear Mom-all,

Well I have fooled around all day and it is almost time to go to bed. I didn't think it was getting so late.

Paul and I went to two Shows this P.M. and this evening, and we are all on K.P. to Morrow. So I don't suppose I will get to write to Morrow Night, as it is usualy about 9:30 until we get done. How is everybody getting along? Did Charles Pass all right in school? Say have you recieved the shoes and watch yet, and how did you Make out with them? O.K. I hope. Say have you heard from Robert?[34] Or do you know his address? If you can get it send it to Me. Well Mom this is awful short but I wrote last Night and thier hasn't Much happened to day, and it is about time for the lights to go out so Must close. With Lots of Love and Kisses to all,

PVT. Meyers

Camp-Fannin
May-30-1944

Dear Mom-all,

Well I survived K.P. yesterday and just got done eating So feel pretty good only we have got to Make up one hour of Bayonet practice we Missed yesterday. It is only an hour and if we didn't have to do that we would be cleaning Machine guns. We fired them to day. I could do better throwing stones than I can shooting it. The ones we have here are about wore out.

Well Mom you sure are fixing up the old shack. I don't see how you do it with the Money you are getting. Well Mom I just go back from Bayonet Practice it wasn't bad our Sargent lives in Tyler and goes home every Night, and he likes to get going early. So we wasn't gone long. Well they have another Rumor going around we call them (Shit house Rumors.) That after our Basic we get 14 days Furlough and then we come back here and they are going to send some of us to Cadre school. To be Corpals and Sargents. Maybe I will get some stripes yet Ha. Ha.

Say Mom you talk about Peeling a little Pan of Potatoes, yesterday Seven of us Peeled 1800 Pounds. Boy I Never saw so Many In My life. And then we had to Slice 900 lbs and Dice the rest. We had a Electric Peeler but we had to cut all the eyes out by hand. But they tasted pretty good. Ha. Ha.

Well Mom we have a big day tomorrow leave at 5:45 A.M. Get back at 5:00 P.M. then tomorrow Night we go out at 9:30 until 12:00. I don't know for sure when we will sleep. We will have to clean automatic Rifles. Well Mom I sure am home sick to see all of you Not only the Kids. I told the Boys the other day I would go over the Hill, But didn't know which way to go. I only know up and down, So I guess I will stay until they tell Me to come home. I don't think it will be very long. So just keep your chin up and I think every thing will be O.K. and don't work to hard, and take care of your self and the Kids the Best you can. I know you will. Must close with Lots of Love and Kisses,

PVT. Meyers

Camp-Fannin
June-1-1944

Dear Mom-all,

Well I was pretty lucky this evening and didn't have to work any after chow only for Myself. Washed out a pair of Fatigues and a pair of leggings. Yesterday Morning we got up at 4:00 A.M. went out about seven Miles and fired the Machine gun. Then came back about 5:00 P.M. ate chow and left again at 7:00 went out about 4 Miles on a Night Problem. Didn't get back until about 12:30. Then I shaved and took a shower before I went to bed. They got big hearted and let us sleep until 6:15 this Morning, and didn't do Much this A.M. and didn't do to Much this P.M. But I suppose we will hit the Ball again Tomorrow. Boy it sure is getting hotter then hell here.

Say did you break your arm or something. I haven't heard from you for two days. Got a letter from Howard yesterday and one from Dad to day. The way Dad wrote I don't think it will be very long before they will have to operate on him for that gland trouble and I expect that will be the end. I do hope it doesn't happen before I get done here, for I would hate to Miss out Now and have to change to another Company, and you have to if you Miss over five days straight.

Well I suppose you think it is about Pay Day again, we got payed last eve. Boy was it a big one. $13.13 Net. Ha. Ha. I won't get Drunk Many times on that do you think? Say I all Most forgot I recieved a letter from Bus. I guess he is in Mississippi. Say did you get the Shoes and watch yet? If I don't hear from them soon I am going to go to town and see about it. Well Mom I think I had better close and get ready for bed, as I am pretty tired and sleepy. So Good Night and The Best of Luck to all. With Lots of Love and Kisses,

PVT. Meyers
P.S. Tell the Kids I said Hello.

Camp-Fannin
June-4-1944

Dear Mom-all,
    Well I suppose you are thinking My arm is broken but it isn't. We have just been to busy, didn't hardly have time to read a letter, let alone writing. It seems like it isn't so hard but we just put in a lot of time. Yesterday Lt. General McNair[35] Commander of the Ground Forces of the U.S. Army was here and Made an Inspection and we had to put on a dress parade Saturday evening. I guess we did all right anyway the Co. Commander said we did and when he says anything good it has to be. Last Saturday we had a Regemental Inspection, and Co. B. was the best all around, except for three fellows that had a pair of shoes in thier Barracks Bag. So we didn't win. He Made them carry thier shoes every place they went for a week. They sure have some funny Punishment. I see about ten or fifteen Men every day carrying thier Rifles every place they go because they are found dirty or drop them or something. So far I haven't had to do anything like that, but I suppose I will before I get out of here, and I don't know when that will be for sure. But I hope it won't be very long. It seems like we don't hear Much about it anymore. Say did you get the Hot water tank fixed up? And have you gotten your check yet? Did Charles Pass O.K.? How did Shirley get along? Did She go to school with him the last day? You ask about the water. It was only about up to our shoulders. And just about the right temperature to go swimming only we had our clothes on and our Packs and Rifles. Some of the fellows fell and went clear under Rifle and all. They sure had a sweet time cleaning them.
    Say is Jett and Kah still on S. Main. I haven't heard from either one for some time, also Killian have only got one letter from him since I have been here. Have been looking for one for a couple of weeks. If I don't hear from him this week, am going to write to him again. Well Mom I think I had better close and go shave and get ready for chow. Paul and I are going to the show this P.M. Write as often as Possible because we sure like to get letters. With Lots of Love and Kisses to all,
    PVT. Meyers

Camp-Fannin
June-5-1944

Dear Mom-all,
    Just a line to let you know I am still alive. Though not feeling so hot this eve, have got a hell of a headache and haven't had anything to drink either. the way I feel I am about ready to start drinking. It sure is getting hot here,

and we have got to March four Miles in the Morning in one hour. If I don't feel it better I don't think I will go. If I can get out of it. You talk about storm it sure does storm a lot here, and is raining like hell right Now has been for about two hours.

Say you don't Need to send My watch Now. Sure glad you got it fixed. Maybe I can use it soon. I hope so anyway. Check it for a few days to see if it is regulated right if it isn't take it back and have them set it right.

Well Mom I heard some More Gossip to day. To the effect that we were to be put on the Reserve list after our Basic. But you can hear Most any thing around here. Well Mom I think I will close and get ready for bed. Maybe I will feel better to Morrow and will write More than. With Lots of Love and Kisses to all.

PVT. Meyers

Camp-Fannin
June-6-1944

Dear Mom-all,

Just a few lines this evening to let you know that I lived through another day, and am feeling fine. Hope every body back home are the same. We had a March this Morning four Miles Made it in 45 Minutes. They sure step us along. But it wasn't as bad as the last one we were on, altho it did bring the sweat out on us. The rest of the day was pretty easy.

Well they finally got the Invasion[36] started, everybody seemed to feel a little better here today. But we would feel a lot better if it was all over so we could get back home for good. It begins to look as if we would be here the full 17 weeks but it seems like the time is passing pretty fast. I guess it is because we are so busy all the time. This is our tenth week Now, only seven to go. They say the last week is only turning in our equipment and getting ready to come home you want to get things ready for we are going to paint the town Red. We will have to celebrate yours and My Birthday. I think I will be home for both at least I hope so.

I don't know for sure but they say that the Goverment pays our expenses to Colombus or some other large town Near home. If they do it won't cost me Much, or I could Thumb a ride from thier home. Ha. Ha. I get enough walking here. I am going to sit on My Fannie all the time I am home. Well Mom I think I had better close and go to bed as it is about time for the lights to go out, so Good Night and Sleep tight, with lots of Love and Kisses to all.

as ever,
PVT. Meyers

Camp-Fannin
June-7-1944

Dear Mom-all,
Just a few lines to let you know I got your letter today and also Shirleys picture. It sure was a good picture of her. When are you going to send Me yours? I could look at it and Maybe it would keep Me from forgetting what you look like. Well Mom I don't know what they are going to do with us. They took up our Kakki caps this evening to put the Braid[37] on them. We aren't supposed to get that until we finish our Basic. I heard last Night that they told one Company in this Battalion that they would leave here before the Next pay day. It can't be to soon for Me.

Well Mom we have to get up an hour early in the Morning. We are going to start out early and get in early at Noon. Tommy Dorsey and his Band is going to play here for one hour at Noon, and we can go hear it if we want to. I think I will sleep. We also have a Night Problem to Morrow Night until 9:30 and Friday Night until Mid Night. Then Saturday we don't start until Noon. But I suppose we will have to get up about 6:15 just the same.

Well how are you getting along with the hot water tank? O.K. I hope. Did you put a faucet in the kitchen? You sure had a hell of a water Bill. But it hadn't ought to be so Much the Next time. Well it is about time for the lights to go out so will close for Now. Good Night and Sleep tight with lots of Love and Kisses to all,
PVT. Meyers

Camp-Fannin
June-8-1944

Dear Mom-all,
Just a few lines this evening before we go out on a Night problem of some kind, to let you know I am still kicking around. Boy is it ever hot we only have one hour to Night. To Morrow Night we leave at 8:00 P.M. until 12:00. Then we are off Saturday A.M. In the Morning we have Inspection. I have been cleaning My Rifle for about an hour and a half. I don't know wether it will Pass or Not. I don't care Much. They want us to take better care of our Rifles then we do ourselves. Got a letter from Lula R. to day. I guess it is really hot in Miss. to. I don't think she is going to stay very long. Also received one from Glenna. She said Pauline broke one of her Toes. I suppose she is in the Hospital with it Ha Ha.

Well how is everything going at home? Fine I hope. We were out to day firing the Mortar that is the gun that shoots shells way out in front of the lines and then blows up. We were firing it at Barrells and Boxes we hit pretty close for Green horns.

How is the weather in Lima? Getting kind of hot I suppose. The way Glenna wrote you are having lots of rain. How is the Garden growing? The

Black Berries are about all gone here and Plums and Peaches are about ripe. The giggers are also doing O.K. and Mosquitos as big as P.38.

Well Mom it is about time to take off so I had better close for to Night, don't suppose I will get to write to Morrow Night. But will if I have time. So Good Night and Sleep tight, with Lots of Love and Kisses to all,
PVT. Meyers

Camp-Fannin
June-11-1944

Dear Mom-all,

Well I suppose you think I have died or something. But I haven't just been to Dam busy to write, haven't hardly had time to take a good Shit.

Somebody ask the Sargent the other day when we were Supposed to Shit. He said only on Sunday the rest of the week let it dry up and blow it out. Boy I can really do that, especially after eating a bunch of these army Beans, which aren't so bad. We only have beans about once a week. Usually on Friday.

Well Mom how are you getting along? O.K. I hope. I am doing about as well as could be expected the way things are. Say you said it was cold back thier. I wish you had some of our heat. It sure is getting hot, and they said it would get about 15° hotter.

This Thursday we March into Tyler and back 18 Miles. I sure hope it isn't very hot that day. These paved roads sure get hot on our feet. And we also have to Carry a Full Field Pack which weighs about 40 Pounds besides our Rifles. Thier are supposed to be 1300 of us parade in town besides the Band. It will be a hell of a Mess I suppose but won't be the first one Ha Ha.

Well Mom it is about time for chow and Paul and I are going to the Show after we eat so will finish later.

Well Mom it is about time to go to bed. We went to the show this afternoon and again this evening. They were both pretty good. Say did you find out what was the Matter with your watch? If you get Mine fixed you can use it until I come home. Well will close for Now, with lots of Love and Kisses to all,
PVT. Meyers

Camp-Fannin
June-12-1944

Dear Mom-all,

Well how is everybody by Now? O.K. I hope. I am feeling O.K. only the dam jiggers and Mosquitos have got us about ate up. We wade and crawl around in the grass so Much and it is just full of them. Did they come after

Lloyd³⁸ yet? And have they caught the Son of a (B) that Raped those girls yet? Say you and Elsie want to be careful until they catch him. Ha. Ha. (Maybe you wouldn't be to hard Raped Now?) Ha. Ha. Well has it warmed up yet? It wasn't so hot here today. It was kind of cloudy and a few Showers, But Not very hard. I hope it is like this Thursday when we March into Tyler. It is 18 Miles round trip, and we have to be in thier at 9:30, leave Camp at 5:30. So we should be thier before it gets very hot.

Say Mom how Many Bonds do we have yet. I wish you would send in a couple and Send Me about $15.00. I would like to buy a Kakhi suit before I come home. We send these to the Laundry and they look like hell. Last week They sent Me someone elses pants, they fit better than the ones I had but they are about wore out. We sure have a time with our clothes. When I come home I will have about four pair of pants for you to shorten. Say thier is a fellow here wrote a Poem about the army life. As soon as I get it copied I will send it to you. Our Sargent read it to day and I thought he would bust him self. If the Company Commander gets a hold of it he would Court Marshall all of us. I suppose He sure is a sour Puss, we always Making fun of him behind his back. But our Sargent is a swell Guy, and we sure get along swell with him. The one that gave me all the hell that day has gone overseas. I sure would like to get a crack at him. If I saw two Japs and him, I would take the first shot at him. Well Mom I think I had better close and drop Bus a line I got a letter from him to day also one from P.S. Killian. Well Good Night to all with Lots of Love and Kisses to all,

as ever-PVT. Meyers

Camp-Fannin
June-14-1944

Dear Mom-all,

Well I have got about 15 Min. until the lights go out so will try to drop you a few lines to let you know I am still on the go. Don't know if I will be tomorrow Night or Not. That is when we go to Tyler. We sure have been busy to Night. We are going in our Kakhi suits with leggings and helmets. We had to wash our leggings and rifle Belts and paint our helmets and I got another G.I. Haircut. I think it will be My last one here. I am going to let it grow on top. If they will let Me. Boy we sure have got a scratching good time here everybody is covered with jiggers. They gave us some stuff to Night to put on them and it sure was hot stuff, for about ten Minutes, but it helped some.

We were out all day to day I suppose we will get another bunch Now. Say I got your pictures to day. They sure are good. But I would a whole lot rather see you in person. I don't think it will be very long. If we are here the full 17 weeks it is only six weeks yet. Some say we go on Bivouac week after Next

that is two weeks and we are here one week after that so you want to have that Money ready to send Me in about four weeks. I don't know for sure but I think they pay our train fare Most of the way. Well Mom it is about time for the lights to go out so will close for Now. Good Night and Sleep tight. I will be thinking of you. With Lots of Love and Kisses to all,
    PVT. Meyers

Camp-Fannin
June-15-1944

Dear Mom-all,

    Well I got back O.K. But it sure was-T.S. in the army that is Tough Shit. And boy was it hot. 102° in the shade and no shade. We left Camp at 6:00 A.M. Got to Tyler about 9:00 then we had to loaf around until 10:00 then we paraded until 12:00. That sure was hot stuff. 3600 Soldiers is some bunch. Thier wasn't that Many came back. They fell out along the road like flies. Thier was about 4 ambulances and 5 or 6 trucks picking them up. The General came along in his car and brought some in with him. It was the toughest thing we have had yet. The C.O. said we did the best of any company that was thier and had the least Men fall out. I think thier was only seven fell out of our Co. of about 200 Men.

    Well Mom how is everything and everybody going at home? Fine I hope. I suppose it is beginning to get pretty hot thier. I know it can cool off here Most anytime will suit Me fine.

    Well Mom are you getting things ready to celebrate when I get home. I don't know for sure the exact day, but I think it will be the first of August or sooner. I am ready to come anytime they let Me. Say I got a Box from Margaurite and Myrtle today, 3 undershirts, 2 handkerchiefs, cigarettes and some chewing gum. Also got a letter from Polly.[39] Well I think I had better close and clean My Rifle and get some rest. I sure Need it. So Goodnight and Best of Luck to all. With Love and Kisses to all,
    PVT. Meyers

Camp-Fannin
June-17-1944

Dear Mom-all,

    Well it is the end of another week and a tough one to. I think it has been the toughest yet. That March and Parade the other day sure took all the Sap out of us. But I think we will recover I didn't even go over to the P.X. or to the show to Night. Did My washing and have got it hung up to dry. I guess it will be dry by Sunday evening. I hope so anyway.

Well how is everything going around Lima? Fine I hope. I suppose it is getting pretty warm Now. It sure is hot here and still heating. I am sitting here with only My shorts on and the sweat is running right down the crack of My xxx. But it cools off a little later in the Night. But we don't have any trouble to keep warm. Is Lloyd still thier? What are they doing about him? Is your Dad still working over at Hooker's? I suppose you fellows are drinking a lot of Beer. I am waiting until I get home. Have only drank one or two bottles since I have been here. Well Mom I think I will close for to Night. Paul and I are going to hunt up a big shade tree in the Morning will write More then. With Lots of Love and Kisses to all.
PVT. Meyers

Camp-Fannin
June-19-1944

Dear Mom-all,

Just a line to let you know I am still alive and kicking around. But it sure is hot. I don't know if we will be able to sleep to Night or Not. I suppose it is getting pretty hot back home to. But I don't think it will get as hot thier as it is here. 2 of the Men in our Platoon had a fit of some kind to day. I guess it was because of the heat. But he is feeling pretty good to Night. I don't know how hot it was but it is getting hotter each day.

You ask when I will be home. I still guess it will be about the first of August. Our Basic will end the 29 of July and we should be out of here in a couple of days.

I guess about the 10th July we go out on Bivouac for two weeks. Then we have one week after that to turn in our equipment that we got here and get our papers fixed up. We have got a hard day to Morrow. We leave camp at 7:00 A.M. and don't get back until 4:00 A.M. Wednesday Morning. Then we don't have to get up until 11:00 and eat dinner. Then we get all afternoon off. But I suppose they will have us Mowing the grass or something. They usually do. Well Mom it is almost time for the lights to go out, so I will close for Now. With Lots of Love and Kisses to all,
PVT. Meyers
P.S. Am sending you that Poem a fellow here wrote.

ARMY-LIFE

1.
The whistle Blows at 5:00 o'clock
Its Drop your cock and Grab a sock
Hit the Floor you Dirty Swine
You Gotta Get up-Rise and Shine

2.
You fumble around and Grab a Shoe
Thinking of all there is to do
And just as you get your Shirt half on
The damned old cannon lets off a Boom

3.
You race like hell for the front Doorway
If your a little late thiers hell to pay
The Sarg yells out, Fall in you clowns
And at last we Make it with an awful Frown

4.
We stand at attention for the actual count
We're reported present with a terrible shout
We're thier in body but Not in Mind
But that's O.K. we're still on time

5.
We run back in and get on the hut
And work like hell with the doors all shut
About the time we get half done
Some one yells chow and here we run

6.
We didn't wash but what the heck
The stuff goes down a rusty neck
We March to the Mess hall and stand in line
And we swallow our Grub in record time

7.
We dash right back to the hut on the Run
We've a pack to roll and the works Not done
We jump around and fight quite a bit
Trying to get time to take a shit

8.
Finally we get our ass on a stool
And just as our Temper is beginning to cool
A whistle blows and here we jump
It's hard as hell to get to take a dump

9.
We run for the door like a bunch of clowns
Fastening straps and buttoning them down
We all (fall in) with the greatest of ease
But that old Sarg is hard to please

10.
He walks around and looks here and there
He sees every packet and uncut hair
The C.O. walks down and looks all around
You can tell he's Mad from his Nasty frown

11.
He says I've got only one thing to say
We don't aim to have any F___ ups to day
Can you hear Me down There?
How about down here?

12.
This is a dam good point I want to Make
Take it or leave it your life's at Stake
You Must take two Salt Pills every Meal
So This Fannin heat you won't be able to feel

13.
He saunters back to the end of the walk
To watch us pass so you'd better Not Balk
(Learn to Pivot Bean) we hear him Growl
Pick up the step Sarg Larson will yell

14.
We count our cadance High and Low
And Road guards out are found to go
We turn left face and right face to
With some one riding the heel of My shoe

15.
We March at attention for about one Mile
When the Sarg yells Route Step with a crooked smile
But all the time our cadance we yell
If you don't sound off you sure catch hell

16.
At last we reach the Neck of a woods
Where we work like hell and try to Make good
We lay on our bellies and Shoot our Gun
And try awful hard to have some fun

17.
We Aim and Point and Fuss and Cuss
Trying to get by without a Mess
And after we've completely lined up our Gun
We FIRE, FIRE, FIRE-But its only a dry Run

18.
We fall out one and zero the Stake
We line our sights and windage take
We squeeze off a shot or two at the Mark
But we've got to hurry to get done before dark

19.
The Non-Coms. Jump and the Lovies dart
Trying to see every Move and Fart
We do very well till the Major appears
By then we're almost ready for tears

20.
The C.O. and all the rest of the class
Jump up and commencing eating our ass
Nothing we do is right they say
And we all think, what a hell of a day

21.
However thiers times when they stop the Race
To give us ten Minutes break in place
But about the time we light up a smoke
Its put em out you dirty Blokes

22.
We then March into the old Drill field
You Need some exercise you dirty heels
So we all stand up in a circular line
We know its coming one at a time

23.
We do the (Bear Walk) and the Indian Dance
And around the ring the whole Bunch Prances
We play leap Frog and Side Straddle hop
Till we think we're found to drop

24.
But the Funniest thing we have to see
Its very cute-Believe you Me
Its Holland doing the walk of a Duck
And Larson Shouting what the F___

25.
After one hour of this or More
We Move to the obstacle course what a Bore
We run and jump and climb the Ropes
And get cussed out because we're such dopes

26.
They March us around for this and that
And which is worse its Hiss and Cat
We get it all before we quit
Without a chance to Piss or Shit

27.
Then when the C.O. is Satisfied Fulley
We finish our job if we've Not been unruly
We all line up and walk left and right
Picking up Butts and everything in sight

28.
At last when we're all to a Frazzle worn
And our ass is dragging and our pants are torn
The whistle blows and we've fall in
And March for the Barracks like 9 kinds of Sin

29.
The Non-Coms follow along at our side
Thier sure is No place in this army to hide
With a pick it up Spillman Get in step Stone
What in hell am I counting for you Bone

30.
When we get to the hut we all make a dash
For the Lister Bar hanging out side by a lash
We had one canteen of water all day
And we're thirsty as a drunk just before pay day

31.
We all March to Supper and come right back
There's Rifles to clean and Details to Crack
We work like hell till half past Nine
Even old Link gets up on the line

32.
Then we Shave and Shower and take a Shit
And by 11:00 oclock the bed we hit
Its been a great day but after it all
We don't give a dam we're on the Ball

33.
We recline ourselves on our stately bed
We aim to rest our bones and head
But the dog tags etc keep twitching
And Cory and Miner both start Bitching

34.
But after awhile we all get quiet
We've got to sleep on this Army Diet
And when its all over and we're at home
We'll never again in this Direction Roam

The End.

Camp-Fannin
June-21-1944

Dear Mom-all,

Well as I lived through yesterday and last Night and got two letters from you to day I will try to drop you a few lines this evening. haven't done Much to day. We got in about 4:00 this Morning ate chow and took a shower got to bed about 5:00 got up at 11:00, cleaned up and ate again. This P.M. all we had to do was clean our equipment and fool around. We go out tomorrow Morning and stay out until Midnight. Then we have the Next Morning off. Boy I sure was all in when we got in this Morning, and I got some More jiggers. Thier sure are a lot of them here and the grass out where we were yesterday is about over our head's. And last Night we were on Patrol practice. And it sure was a Mess, trees and Brush I don't believe I could get through at all in daytime. All we had to go by was a compass, and I was the Patrol leader, and had to lead the way, fell in a ditch once and about broke My Neck.

Say what did you think of the Poem I sent you? It is about as Near this shit as anyone could describe. Well Mom it is about time to eat so will finish after a while. Well chow is over and work all done and ready for bed-so will finish and call it a day. How are you and the kids getting along? Fine I hope. I expect to see you all in about five or six weeks. I suppose that seems like a long time to you. But it seems like the time is going pretty fast to us. I dont know what they are going to do with us after that. They say No one over 30 years of age goes over seas. And I sure as hell don't want to stay here, so maybe they will let us know some of these days. I did hear that some were being trained for M.P. don't know where they would send us. Well Mom I can't think of anything else to write so will close for Now. With Lots of Love and Kisses to all.

as ever-PVT. Meyers

Camp-Fannin
June-23-1944

Dear Mom-all,

Well I guess I had better drop you a few lines this evening to let you know I am still alive and Marching around in the hot sun. I wish it was 58° here for about five weeks. We were out last Night until about 11:30. And not wolfing around either but we didn't do Much work. They sent Me to the dentist yesterday Morning, didn't get out of thier until Noon. They filled one tooth and cleaned all of them. I never knowed I had a hollow tooth until then. They are fixing everyones teeth before we go on Bivouac, which is only two weeks. I sure will be glad when I can get home for a few days at least and a whole lot glader when I can get home to stay.

I got a letter from Mousa to day. I guess they are having a hell of a time with the Busses. He said that some of them didn't run all the time because they couldn't get drivers. I hope old Duncan has to go out and push them around. I think he could have got Me a Deferment if he would have tried. When I come home I am going to talk to him and if I happen to get Mad I am going to tell him what I think of him. I got a letter from Kah yesterday he said young Carl had left that day. If they keep on all of the old Drivers will be gone. It's a wonder he hasn't hired some women to drive, or has he. Well how is the weather up thier by Now? Warmer I hope. It is plenty hot here and we have got a big day to Morrow have to get up at 4:00 leave Camp at 5:45 got about 7 Miles to March out to the machine gun range. I think this week just about finishes up on our firing on the range. I hope so anyway. Sure am getting tired cleaning guns and Rifles. I sure will be glad to get rid of this M.1. when I get home to stay. I am going to buy one and just put it out in the yard and let it rust. Well Mom tell Elsie I have got My Rifle cleaned and I have got to close and take a shower, and get ready to hit the hay. So Good Nightie. Wish I was home to hit the hay in a good bed. With Lots of Love and Kisses to all,
PVT. Meyers

Camp-Fannin
June-25-1944

Dear Mom-all,

Will try to drop you a few lines to let you know I got your letter and Elsies Picture and the jiggers are about all gone, of course I don't know wether that is what done it or Not. Your guess is as good as Mine but I have My own opinion.

Well how is the weather back in Lima? I wish it would get a little cooler out here. It sure is hot. But I think the worst is past at least I hope so. We were out on the range yesterday firing the Machine gun. I was on the ammunition detail in the P.M. and the rest of the Company left before we got done so I got to ride in on the truck. It was My first ride since I came here, and I had to go out this P.M. to help do some work on the range. They took us out and brought us back in a truck. They sure have got some crazy dam drivers here. I wouldn't let one of them push a wheel Barrow for Me, Let alone a truck. But I guess I aint running the army, at least they don't ask Me for advice.

What is your dad doing Now? I don't suppose he could get his job back at the picture Show or don't he want it? I suppose that is a hot place in the summer, or is it air conditioned Ha. Ha. I suppose about like these huts. Hot in summer. Cold in winter. Have you been over to see Dad yet? How is Lula? Better I hope? I suppose you have got your house cleaning done and taking it easy Now. I got a letter from Dad. He wanted Me to try and get him as a dependent, Said he could get $50 a Month. I don't think I could do it Now, as I didn't put his Name down when I came in the army, and our Commanding Officer is leaving this week. I don't know who is going to take his place, and I don't think I will try it while I am here. Because when they get ready to send us home I sure want to be ready to hit the road. And hit it fast this place has got Me dam Near Nuts, or was I before? Well Honey I think I had better close for Now as I want to write to Bus. With Loads of Love and Kisses to all. I remain as ever,

PVT. CE Meyers

P.S. Tell Elsie I have had My Shave-Shower and Shit. Ha. Ha.

Camp-Fannin
June-26-1944

Dear Mom-all,

Just a line this evening to let you know I recieved the shoes and Money order and Thanks a lot. I put the shoes on this evening and felt like I could fly after wearing these G.I. Shoes and I polished and Shined them all up. They don't look half bad. It will just be a little More work, But it sure will be worth it.

Say Mom what do you think about selling that house and buying some where else. If you can try and see Ben Ogle and see what he can do for us. Maybe he can get it set and when I get home we can finish the deal. I sure would like to get out of that end of town, as it will be worse after this is over and we could get More out of it Now.

Has Steve heard anymore from the draft Board? I sure hope he doesn't have to go, as he can help out a whole lot. Have they came after Lloyd yet?

Well Mom it is only a little over four weeks yet until we finish here, and then for a big Boom. I sure wish that Carrol and Bus could be thier. Say did

you ever hear where Jackie Mulching went or where Bob is? I have been going to ask you, But Never thought about it when I went to write. How is Al and Vondeta[40] Making it? Do they ever come out anymore? I don't expect I will get to see half of the people I would like to. Well Must close for Now. With Love and Kisses to all,
    PVT. Meyers

Camp-Fannin
June-27-1944

Dear Mom-all,

Well we got another day in, and it was pretty soft. But we have got a hard one ahead. Get up at 4:00 A.M. in the Morning, leave Camp at 5:15 have got 7½ Miles to March out to the Rifle Range. I think it is our last day firing the M.1. Rifle, we finished up on the Machine Gun yesterday. Sure Glad of it. We had to clean them every Night only 125 of them. Next week we turn in our old Rifles and get brand New ones to finish our Basic, which won't be long.

Well Mom how is everybody at home by Now? Fine I hope. Say I Might go to town Sunday. If I do will try to find a little present of some kind for Shirley. Suppose I had better get one for Charles to. Also Mother. Ha. Ha. I don't know for sure wether I will get any new clothes or Not-they say we get New ones when we leave here. So I think I will wait a while and see. Have they taken Lloyd back yet? Where is My Dad at? Still over to Howard's? Well Mom it is getting dark and Paul and I are laying out on the lawn so will close for Now. With Lots of Love and Kisses to all. PVT. Meyers

Camp-Fannin
June-29-1944

Dear Mom-all,

Just a few lines this evening to let you know I am still alive and on K.P. tomorrow. One of the other companies in this Battalion are out on a Night problem to Night and will be in a[t] 4:00. So we have to get up at 2:15 so we can fed them before they go to bed. But our company has Inspection tomorrow and a Night problem tomorrow Night, we get out of both so I don't Mind so Much.

Well Mom I don't know what the Dictionary says about Bivouac. But you can keep on writing, as they bring our Mail out every day, and also pick up our Mail we write. They even send a barber out to cut our hair but I guess it is pretty tough. We have to crawl under a Barbed wire entanglement and they fire a Machine gun over our heads. Boy I sure am going to hug the ground when I go through. But the Bulletts are about two or three feet over our heads. I am going to get Me some powder of some kind to keep the jiggers and Mosquitos off. I guess they are about the worst thing we have to contend with.

Say Mom have you been getting your checks regular? I have been wondering about it, and you Never said anything about it. I don't know wether I will Need Much Money to come home on or Not, as they say we will Shipped out as soon as we get done. And I think they will pay our way to Chicago or Cincinnati. And it won't cost Much from thier. Got a letter from Bus to day. He said he had heard they were going to change that school where he was at to Ohio State at Colombus. That sure would be a break for him. I haven't got the least Idea what they are going to do with us. They say this camp is going to be turned into a Prison of war Camp. If it is I suppose a lot of Men will be left here. I hope I am Not one of them. They are also picking out some Men for Cadre. I don't want None of that either. I am pretty dam Particular. I would like to go to Fort Amanda. Ha. Ha. Well Mom I think it is about time to sign off and get some sleep. This is going to be a short Night. So Good Night and Sleep tight. With Loads of Love and Kisses to all.

I remain yet, PVT. C.E. Meyers

Camp-Fannin
July-2-1944

Dearest Mom-all,

Well I suppose you think the heat has got Me or something. But it hasn't. Friday we went on K.P. from 2:45 A.M. until 9:00 P.M. I was so dam tired I didn't think I would get to the Hut. And until I got cleaned up it was to late, and yesterday didn't have time. Paul and I came to town this Morning to get away from camp for awhile. We are at the U.S.O. Now. I guess we will go back to camp about 3:00 as I have got some work to do, didn't do anything this Morning before we left.

Well honey how is everybody and everything going at home? Fine I hope. It is about the same here. It sure Must be hot thier. It is a little cooler here the last three or four days. We had a little rain last Night. The first in three weeks. It sure is dry. I think that is what Makes it so hot.

Say did that woman Buy Hooker out? Tell your Dad I said for him to be careful. I have been looking around for something for Shirley. The stuff sure is picked over. I don't know if I can find her any thing or Not. If I don't tell her I will bring her something when I come home also you and Charles.

Paul and I had our pictures taken in a cow boy outfit, am sending them to you to keep the rats and Negroes away. Ha. Ha. By the way How are Colored folks out in that end getting along. I hope to all cut each others throats, and I suppose you do to. Have you had Shirley shot yet? And are the Kids home

Now? I sure am anxious to see you all. Now they have got Me talking like these Southerners or hill Billies.

Say you know that Show you said you Saw Back Home in Indiana. Paul and I and a fellow from Indiana went to see it last Night. He said it Made him so home sick he had a Notion to go A.W.O.L. But he came to town with us today feeling a little better Now. I sure was feeling like that Friday on K.P. But it don't do a fellow any good, and a letter from home sure helps to keep up a guys spirits. Got a letter from Glenna yesterday. The way she wrote I took it for granted that Charlie is still helling around. Any one like that ought to be in this camp awhile. He would know what a home Meant in a short time. And I'll bet he would settle down, and stay at home when he got a chance. She also said he wasn't working all the time.

Say is My Dad still at Howard's? The last letter I got from him he was expecting to go over to Sollies as soon as Lula got better. I have an Idea that will be along time. Well Honey this is about all the gossip for Now, so will close for today. With all My Love and Kisses to all. I remain your faithful Husband and Daddy.

PVT. Meyers

Camp-Fannin
July-4-1944

Dearest Mom-all,

Well I suppose you are all celebrating the 4th to day. We sure have this P.M. We were out until Mid Night last Night. So was off about all A.M. Just went to a picture show and had a test. Then they issued us each a New Rifle, and gave us the after Noon off to clean the grease off of them. I started at 1:00 P.M. and got done at 4:30. Paul and I are going to a stage show to Night. It is called Pin ups and Peanut Girls. I don't know what it is like But they gave us passes to go, so won't be out Much but our time. And that don't Mean Much here.

Say I was just wondering if you remembered Six years ago today? We sure had some hot games, didn't we? I haven't played for so long I don't suppose I can play anymore.

Well how is the weather in the big city? Still pretty hot I suppose and still heating. But before you know it the snow will be flying again. I sure hope this dam war is over before then. I don't think it can last very Much longer.

Say Honey I didn't get Shirley anything for her Birthday. But will try to find something for each of you before I come home. I have a couple More of those bunches of cards like I sent before. I am going to send each of the kids one. What do you want for your Birthday? I don't know what I could get here. But I think Maybe I will get home just about that time and will get you something. All I want for Mine is to be home. Boy that would be the best present I could ever get, and about all a fellow could ask for. Well Mom it is about chow time so will close for Now. I don't know wether I will get to write to Morrow or Not as we have another Night problem until 12:00 so until then. With all My Love and Kisses to all. I remain as ever,

PVT. Meyers

Camp-Fannin
July-7-1944

Dearest Mom-all,

Well will try to drop you a few lines this evening to let you know I am still alive. I suppose you think I have broken My arm. I had began to think you had. We have been going about all the time. But Not doing Much either. We have been trying to get our old Rifles cleaned up and turned in, and every spare Minute we had we have to work on them. I just got Mine passed. Now I have only one which is one to Many.

Well how is everybody and everything back home? Fine I hope. We sure are all looking forward to seeing our families soon. I sure wish it was for good. But Maybe it won't be for long, at least I hope it won't be. Boy I sure would like to have some good old Ham and egg's, all the eggs we get are scrambled or fryed hard and usually cold. And scrambled I just can't go them very often. This Morning we got up and Made a 3 Mile force March before breakfast. Boy was I hungry. I think I could have eaten Most anything and liked it.

How did Shirley act on her Birthday? or was she down to Lulas? I suppose she was disappointed because I didn't send her any thing. But I will bring her something when I come home. What did they say about the cards? I didn't look at them Much before I got ready to send them, and they wasn't so hot for the kids. How is the Garden doing? I suppose it helps a lot to fill the table. I sure could go for some good old home cooking. But it seems like I am holding My own, weight 182. Which isn't bad for Me in this hot weather and all the work we do? they say that during our Basic here we will walk 1785 Miles besides what we do on our own. Well Honey I have got a lot of work to do. So I think I had better close for Now. Will try to write oftener after this so with all My Love and Kisses to all. I remain as ever your faithful Daddy.

PVT. Meyers

Camp-Fannin
July-9-1944

Dearest Mom-all,

Well I guess I am all ready to go on Bivouac at least am going to call it done. We sure are busy, getting all our clothes washed and our packs Made up. Now Mom don't forget to write often, as I think we will Need a lot to keep up our Moral out in that God forsaken place. One of the Boys just came in that has been out thier getting things ready he said the Mosquitos we[re] sure thick. But they gave each of us two bottles of stuff to keep them off. I also got some stuff to keep the jiggers off. I hope it works, if it don't all I will get done on My Furlough is scratch.

Well Honey how is everything going in the big city? Fine I hope. It has been about the same here. I hope to get back to see how everything is going very soon. We had a physical exam this week. They finally found out I had the (Piles) Ha. Ha. I don't know what they will do about them. They haven't bothered Me since I have been in this Dam army. Well Honey it is about chow time so will close until after I eat.

Well Mom just got done feeding My face and feel pretty good Now. Had Roast Pork, Mashed potatoes, Gravy, Corn, and Salad, also orange juice and cake. Some days the eats are pretty good, others they are rotten as hell. I sure will be glad to get home and get some good old home cooking. But I guess it won't be long, at least I hope Not.

Say Mom do you know who bought the Restaurant at Waynesfield? Paul said his wife wrote that Smith had sold out but didn't say who to. I suppose they will have a big time if we all get home at once. But I don't know if I will be able to take it anymore. It sure has been along time since I took on anything stronger than coffee. Ha. Ha. Well Mom I think I had better close for Now. Don't know when I will get a chance to write again. But I think we will get to write almost every day. So until later Good bye to all, and good Luck. With all My Love and Kisses to all.

PVT. Meyers

Camp-Fannin
July-13-1944

Dearest Mom-all,

Well I am still alive, Believe it or Not. They sure have been keeping us on the ball. it is 7:00 A.M. Now and we haven't been in bed since yesterday Morning at 6:00 A.M. Monday we got up at 5:00 A.M. and got to bed at 6:30 A.M. Tuesday Morning, And got up at 10:30, left again at 1:00 P.M. and got in at 12:30. So you can see why I haven't written before. I guess I should be in bed Now, but was afraid if I didn't write you would disown Me for good. Received three letters from you yesterday also one from Bus. Am Not going to answer his until I get back to camp. So if you write to him be sure to tell him why I don't answer.

Well how is everything going in the big city? Fine I hope. The time sure is going fast here it seems like. I guess it is because we are on the go all the time. We don't have time to realize what day it is. The things we are doing isn't so hard, it is just long days. But I suppose it is going awful slow to you, especially when you don't get any letters for a few days.

Say that woman that Bought out Hooker's place is the woman that Red and Etta always talked about and Mamie worked for when dad was sick.

Well Honey I guess I had better close and get a little sleep as we have to get up at 9:30. I don't know when we will get to bed again. Say Mom you can send Me that Money about the 20th send a Money order, and I can keep it until I get ready to use it. Well Honey until later will close. With all My Love and Kisses to all. As ever,

PVT. Meyers

Camp-Fannin
July-16-1944

Dearest Mom-all,

Well as it is Sunday and I have got all the work done, I will try to drop you a few lines again to let you know I am still alive after a pretty wild day yesterday. We crawled under the Machine Gun fire and had some work in village fighting. Sure fired a lot of rounds and they were real.

Well how is everybody by Now? Fine I hope. I am O.K. only hungry as hell. Since we have been out here I have ate everything but My Shoes and am about ready to start on them Next. We have had pretty good eats so far. They say we are going to have chicken for dinner, and we are having a party this evening. The company is putting it on. 30 cases of Beer, Coco Cola, and Sandwiches. I think I will drink a couple of Bottles. My first since we have been here.

Well Honey the time is going pretty fast, only two More weeks. Boy I sure will be glad to get home for at least a few days anyway. I don't know just the exact day, But will try to let you know for sure soon. If Nothing else, will send a telegram along the way If I get a chance. I have an Idea we will come to Chicago and transfer from there home. Maybe Cincinnati.

Say Honey I told you to send Me that Money. I didn't Mean it all. $50 will be enough and what I don't use I will give you back. You ask about it I bought a uniform. I found out that all we can buy is just like the ones we have, and we only get two of them. So I don't think I will buy any Now until I see for sure. Say I almost fergot to tell you I went to church this Morning. Boy I sure am getting good don't you think so? Well Honey just got done eating and feel pretty good only it is pretty hot, and thier isn't Much shade, just little Pine trees, which don't Make Much shade, only they are better than None. Well Honey I think I had better close for Now, as it is about time to drink the Beer. And I don't want to Miss out on anything that is free in the army. Will try to write a little oftener this week. So be good and Good-Bye for Now. With all My Love and Kisses to all,

PVT. Meyers

Camp-Fannin
July-17-1944

Dearest Mom-all,
    Well as I have a little time yet before dark will try to drop you a few lines for we have a Night problem tomorrow Night and don't suppose I will get to write then. We had it pretty easy today and got in at 5:00. We ate chow and went down and took a shower. Came back and Shaved and cleaned My Rifle and Now am going to rest until time to turn in.
    How is everything going in the big city? Fine I hope. Did Shirleys vaccination take? I hope so, So you don't have to take her back. Is the Boys still down to Lula's? I got a letter from her a while back. But I don't think I ever answered it. I don't intend to write Many More letters while I am here. Just to you, and I May write to Dad when we get back to camp. It sure is hard to write or anything else out here. We had our party yesterday evening. Beer, Coca Cola and Sandwiches they also had a little Music. All we lacked was the women, The Most important part. Ha. Ha. Well Honey it is getting pretty dark so will close for Now. With all My Love and Kisses to all.
    PVT Meyers

Camp-Fannin
July-20-1944

Dearest Mom-all,
    Well as I have a little time before we have to go and see a show of some kind will try to drop you a few lines again. Just received your letter of the 17th. Sure glad to hear from you. I suppose you got tired looking for a letter from Me, since we have been out here. We don't have Much time but I guess the first Platoon are going back to camp to Morrow Night, and the rest of the company Saturday Morning. I am ready to go Now if they will let Me. But I don't suppose they will, as we have a pretty busy day to Morrow, also yesterday. We left camp at 6:30 A.M. and got back at 2:30 this Morning, and got up at 7:00. I figure on sleeping all the way home. They had us sign a slip the other day for our Transportation. The way they talked we will shipped some place in Maryland. All it will cost Me will be from Colombus O. to Lima and back, which won't be Much about $4 or $5 at the Most.
    How is your Dad getting along over at the Beer Joint? I suppose Red and Etta hang out over thier, as they were always such good friends. I got a letter from Pauline to day. Did you see the piece in the Paper about her brother. She copied it off and sent it to Me. I don't know what date it was in.
    Well Honey I don't know exactly what day I will be home, but I think we will have time to let you know for sure. Well Honey will close for Now. Will write a good letter when I get back to camp Saturday. So until then with all My Love and Kisses to all.
    PVT. Meyers

Camp-Fannin
July-23-1944

Dearest Mom-all,
Well we finally got back to camp. Sure glad of it to. We came in Saturday Morning got here about 11:00. All we did the rest of the day was clean up ourselves and equipment. It sure was a job, everything full of sand. I have gotten everything cleaned and all My clothes washed except a few. I am going to to send to the Laundry to day. Well how is the fishing? Are you using My New fishing Rod? And How does it work? I Never did catch a fish on it.

Well Honey I got the Money order Saturday it will be plenty. And I can give you back some of it when I get home. Unless I take a Notion to go on a sphree before I get thier and I don't think I will. Well Honey I don't know what Rail Road I will come in on it all depends when I get off. They told us we could get off at any town Nearest our home if the train stopped thier. But as we have to go to Colombus to catch the train to go back I think it would be best to get off thier, so I will know what the connections will be and what time I will have to be thier, or Maybe I could do like Junior and take My time and leave whenever I want to. Ha. Ha.

Paul Spillman just came in and payed Me back a dollar he borrowed off of Me. He just got back from town. His wife sent his Money by telegram and he had to go to town to get it. I still have My Money order. Am Not going to get it cashed until I get ready for it, and then I won't spend it. For when they say go I am going to be on My way. I think we will come Most of the way on Troop train. Maybe to St. Louis. But from thier on I have an Idea we will come by Passenger. The Route I have in Mind we will go through Sindey and Bellefontaine if they do, I am going to get off thier. Well Honey this is about all the gossip for Now so will close for Now. But will try to write a little oftener this week. So with all My Love and Kisses to all. I Remain as ever,
PVT. Meyers

Camp-Fannin
July-24-1944

Dearest Mom-all,
Well I don't suppose you will know how to act if I get to writing regular again. But will try to drop you a few lines anyway. We had a pretty soft day to day. I think it will be the rest of the week at least I hope so. Maybe I will be in pretty good shape when I get home, and won't want to sleep all the time.

We had our final Physical examanation also Dential today. Don't know for sure how we came out. And don't suppose we will until we get our shipping orders some say we will get them the last of this week. I sure hope so. I hope to get home for your Birthday. But I doubt if I Make it. We had an Inspection this evening to see if we had everything that was issued to us. Strange to say I have it all yet. I was short one cap. But found a fellow that had two, so he gave Me one of them. I think it was Mine to start with.

Well Honey I only drank four Beers and it didn't taste very good at that. We are going to have another Party one Night this week. It costs each of us a dollar. That will Make about $200. We should get a lot of Beer. Don't you think we are also going to have Pop and sandwiches. I think it will be Thursday evening as we have Friday about all day off. All we have to do is clean up our stuff. Boy I sure will be glad to get real clothes again, at least for a few days. Well Honey I think I had better close and write a letter to Bus or he will Disown Me as his Pop. Ha. Ha. So until later with Lots of Love and Kisses. I remain as ever,

PVT. Meyers

NOTES

1. Steve was Carl's brother-in-law, the husband of Florence's sister Elsie.
2. This was a form of guard duty to stoke the furnaces during cold weather.
3. Etta was Carl's sister.
4. Elsie was Florence's sister, Steve was Elsie's husband, and Dick was their son.
5. These are men from Waynesfield, Ohio.
6. The Army regularly provided entertainment for the trainees, usually a movie.
7. Bill Kaufman, Carl's nephew.
8. Bus was Florence's nephew, the son of Lula, Florence's sister.
9. Glenna was Carl's sister.
10. Myrtle was Carl's sister-in-law, Florence's sister.
11. These shows were most likely training films.
12. These were periodic tests on military matters such as courtesy and how and when to salute officers.
13. See chapter 1 for an explanation of the Replacement Training Centers.
14. These men were friends from Lima.
15. Wapakoneta, Ohio, in Auglaize County, southwest of Waynesfield.
16. A place to play cards back home.
17. Howard was Carl's brother.
18. Lula was Carl's sister-in-law, Florence's sister.
19. Standing retreat was taking down the flag at the end of the day.
20. Rationing stamps.
21. This was an acquaintance from home.
22. Carroll Wallace, Carl's nephew.
23. Myrtle was Carl's sister-in-law, Florence's sister, and Sam was her husband; Margaurite was their daughter and Carroll Wallace's wife.
24. To repeat parts of basic training.
25. A bus driver with whom Carl worked in Lima.
26. Betty was the wife of Bus, Carl's nephew.
27. Buck was a nickname for Carl's son Charles.
28. An overnight training exercise.

29. This was one of several types of boxed meals the soldiers ate, which today are called MREs. During World War II the C Ration consisted of ten small cans of meat and vegetables (meat and beans, meat and vegetable stew, meat and spaghetti, ham, eggs, and potatoes, meat and noodles, meat and rice, frankfurters and beans, pork and beans, ham and lima beans, chicken and vegetables) along with crackers, jam, powdered drinks, sugar, and cereals. The K Ration was also a boxed meal that was marked either breakfast, dinner, or supper. Breakfast consisted of a fruit bar, Nescafe, sugar, crackers, and a small tin of ham and eggs. Dinner and supper included a can of cheese or potted meat, crackers, orange or lemon powder, sugar, chocolate, and chewing gum. For more on the other boxed meals, see George Forty, *US Army Handbook 1939-1945* (NY: Barnes & Noble Books, 1998 reprint of 1979 original), 117-119.
30. This was another bus driver from Lima.
31. This was a training exercise.
32. Ruth Killian was a family friend from Lima.
33. Carl Seaman was Florence's older brother.
34. Robert was Carl's younger brother.
35. Lieutenant General Lesley J. McNair was commander of Army Ground Forces (AGF) from 1942 until 1944. He was killed in Normandy during Operation COBRA on July 25, 1944.
36. This was D-Day, the invasion of Normandy on June 6, 1944.
37. The company or regimental colors.
38. Lloyd was Florence's brother.
39. Polly was Carl's sister-in-law, married to Carl's brother Walter.
40. These were friends from Lima.

Chapter Three

In the European Theater of Operations

Private Carl Meyers and his fellow trainees completed their work at Camp Fannin at the end of July 1944 and went home on furlough. His final letter from Texas was dated July 24, 1944, so presumably Meyers was home in Lima, Ohio by the beginning of August. After 17 weeks of basic training, it must have been a welcome change to be a civilian for a few weeks. He most certainly relaxed, visited with friends and family, and celebrated the short time he had before receiving his overseas orders. If he did not already know or guess, Meyers soon learned that he would be going to Europe, and he was ordered to Fort Meade, in Baltimore, Maryland.

Fort George G. Meade, named for the Civil War general, was one of two installations designated a replacement depot by the U.S. Army Ground Forces in 1943 (the other was Fort Ord, California). With a capacity of 18,000, Fort Meade began its new mission in August 1943.[1] Replacement depots were essentially staging grounds for newly-trained soldiers in preparation for their travel to an overseas theater of operation. The soldiers' stay at the depot ranged from several days to a couple of weeks, and while there Army officials made sure they were adequately prepared. Troops underwent a physical examination (including more inoculations), were checked for proficiency with their primary weapon, and in general were qualified to board a troop transport and proceed overseas. In some cases, if their equipment was already crated for shipment, the soldiers participated in other training maneuvers, such as abandon ship or gas chamber exercises. The men had to be kept active in order to maintain their physical conditioning, discipline, and to help build morale. As the date of embarkation neared, the troops were not permitted to leave the base, make telephone calls, or have visitors.

When the time came for troops to leave the replacement depot, they boarded trains for the trip to the port of embarkation (in some cases the train went right up to the pier). At this point, tracing Meyers's movements becomes a little blurry. He mentioned being at Fort Meade in his October 15, 1944 letter (after arriving in Europe), but nowhere did he elaborate on his travel overseas. The records of vessels used to transport troops to theaters of operation were destroyed in 1951, so there is no official record of which vessel transported Meyers to Europe. Attempting to identify the vessel was an exercise in eliminating ships based upon information in Meyers's letters. From Fort Meade he boarded a vessel at a port of embarkation, traveled to England, marched across that country, and ended up in France. With this information, it seems likely that he sailed to England aboard either the *Mauretania* or *Mariposa*. The former left New York on August 24, 1944 and arrived in Liverpool on August 31, 1944. The latter left Boston on August 30, 1944 and arrived in Liverpool on September 7, 1944. His first letter from Europe was September 11, 1944.[2] If he sailed on the *Mauretania*, it would have been almost two weeks after landing that he penned his first correspondence. Based upon the frequency of his letters during basic training, this seems remote. More likely, he boarded the *Mariposa*, which docked on September 7, and found time to write home just a few days later. Regardless of the vessel, by early September 1944, Meyers was in France.[3]

The trip from the port of embarkation to Europe was probably no joyride for Private Meyers. Living in landlocked Ohio, his experience with large ocean-going vessels was certainly limited, probably nonexistent. Accommodations were cramped, to say the least. Soldiers slept below deck on canvas and metal frame bunks (similar to a hammock) stacked six high, with perhaps two feet of space between them. There were so many bunks that there was virtually no place to sit or stretch. Soldiers were normally permitted on-deck during daylight hours, but after dark were relegated below deck. Troops were fed twice a day and fresh drinking water was limited. Rumors that officers received better food and roomier sleeping accommodations made tempers short; fistfights on troopships were commonplace. These living conditions, combined with the monotony of the trans-Atlantic voyage, probably made most soldiers, Meyers included, feel relieved to disembark on foreign soil, despite the dangers that awaited them.

Much like a soldier's time in basic training, mail was of utmost importance when he was overseas. Historian Gerald Linderman wrote that mail from home "gained an extraordinary prominence" in the American military. Noted war correspondent Ernie Pyle echoed those sentiments in one of his columns when he wrote, "The two best morale boosters were the *Stars and Stripes* and letters from home." In a similar vein, Bill Mauldin, soldier-turned-cartoonist, wrote that, "A soldier's life revolves around his mail."[4] Because of the potentially large volume of correspondence crossing the oceans, the Postal Service, in conjunction with the War and Navy departments, created Victory Mail, or V-mail as it was more commonly known.

Launched on June 15, 1942, V-mail was a system to reduce the volume of correspondence in and out of the country in order to save space on naval vessels, space that was needed for war materials. In using V-mail, correspondents wrote on a single sheet of paper that doubled as the envelope when folded. That sheet was then reproduced on 16mm microfilm, and only the microfilm was transported overseas. After crossing the ocean (Atlantic or Pacific), the microfilmed letters were printed on 4-inch by 5-inch pieces of paper and sent out for delivery. In this way, space on ships was greatly reduced; 150,000 one-page letters would fill 37 mail bags, but it required only one sack when microfilmed into V-mail. By November 1, 1945, almost 1.25 billion pieces of V-mail had been delivered.[5] Private Meyers utilized V-mail, as all of his correspondence from Europe was in this form.

Another drastic difference in writing from a theater of operation was that the soldiers' mail was censored, something not done during basic training. For security reasons, every letter a soldier wrote home from Europe or the Pacific was read by an officer before it was mailed. This was done to ensure that sensitive information did not leak out to the public, no matter how harmless it may seem to the soldier writing the letter. For example riflemen, particularly if they were on the front lines, could not disclose to family back home where they were. Meyers demonstrated this in his October 5, 1944 letter when he wrote, "Well will drop you a few lines again to let you know I am still at the same place, and getting along just fine, altho I can't tell you the

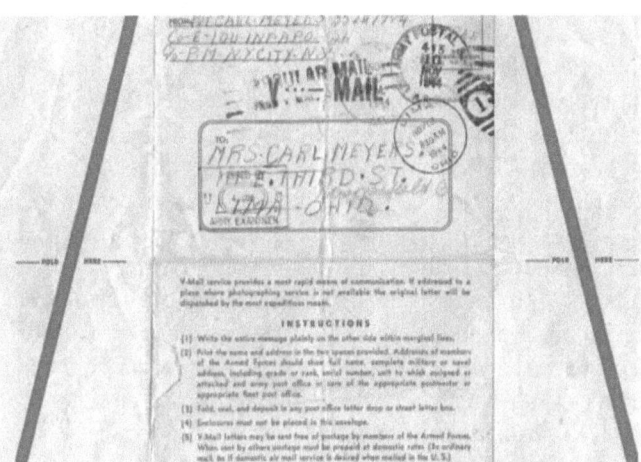

An example of World War II V-mail. Notice the instructions and the indications of where to fold the letter. These letters were microfilmed and transported to America for delivery. This letter was dated November 4, 1944, the final letter Carl Meyers wrote. Photo in possession of the authors.

Name of the place or where it is." At that time, Meyers was not on the front lines and had yet to be assigned to a unit. The Army took careful security measures to ensure important information was not accidentally disclosed to anybody.

When Carl Meyers went to the European Theater of Operations (ETO) in the fall of 1944, he was not attached to a specific Army unit (regiment, division, army), but rather as an individual soldier in the Army's replacement system. The replacement system was the Army's plan to keep units at the front at full strength. The Army decided early on in the war to create only a limited number of divisions; those units, particularly in the ETO, would remain at the front lines until the war ended. Even when their numbers were reduced by casualties, these units were not sent behind the lines for rest and to receive reinforcements. Instead, individual soldiers, called replacements, were sent to the front lines to keep units at or near full strength; U.S. Chief of Staff George Marshall believed the replacement system was the best way to keep units at full strength without taking them off of the front lines. Replacements did not train together, and often arrived at the front at night in the middle of a campaign or battle. They typically did not know anybody in the unit (squad, platoon, company), and had to be taught the rudiments of survival at the front. Historian Russell Weigley described the replacement's arrival at the front this way: "Too often the system of individual replacements flung a lone man into a group of strangers, with no chance to get to know them before he entered combat with them. Too often, the replacement arrived at night and did not even see his comrades' faces before the battle resumed." Stephen Ambrose wrote that replacements arrived at the front "unknown, unknowing, scared, bewildered, untrained." Gerald Linderman quoted a soldier who described the typical replacement's experience after joining a unit: "You go up as a replacement and your chances are awful. The men who are there are all friends, they feel responsible for each other, they'll do anything to save each other. That means every dirty, dangerous job they hand right over to the replacements. The Sergeants don't even bother to learn your name. They don't want to know anything about you…You go into a new Company, all by yourself, and you'll be on every patrol, you'll be the point of every attack."[6] Most replacements probably felt a sense of isolation after being assigned to a unit and being brought to the front.

The replacement system was a way to keep Army divisions at full strength, or near full strength, and on the front lines continuously without interruption. What that meant for the individual rifleman was that he remained at the front until the war ended or he suffered a wound that took him out of combat (either temporarily or permanently). There was almost no chance for any unit to be permitted time behind the lines to receive reinforcements or to train replacements. The result was an astronomical turnover rate in the frontline rifle divisions in the ETO. The 1st Infantry Division, for example, experienced a 205% turnover rate from June 1944 until May 1945; likewise, the 29th Division had a 204% turnover rate and the 4th Division 252%.[7]

Historians have generally criticized and condemned the replacement system. Peter Mansoor called the replacement system "flawed," Stephen Ambrose suggested that it was "criminally wasteful," and Michael Doubler described the "adverse effects" it had on morale, discipline, and training.[8] Russell Weigley noted that despite all the faults in the system, it was preferable to those other nations used.[9] Samuel Stouffer and his team of investigators examined the replacement system from the perspective of social scientists rather than from the purely military perspective. They addressed the assimilation of the replacement into a veteran unit, the "career" of a replacement soldier, and the combat effectiveness of replacements. Though Stouffer did not draw a definitive conclusion on the merits of the system, he identified numerous issues replacements faced.[10] Clearly the replacement system was not an ideal method to reinforce units on the front lines and keep them at full strength, but this was an issue the American armed services have struggled with in every major conflict. Regardless of the drawbacks and flaws in the system, Private Meyers entered the ETO as a replacement soldier, a rifleman waiting to be assigned to a combat unit.

In order to process the replacement soldiers, to funnel them to combat units, Army Ground Forces (AGF) established a series of depots throughout the ETO, and Meyers went through several of them. Like most replacements,

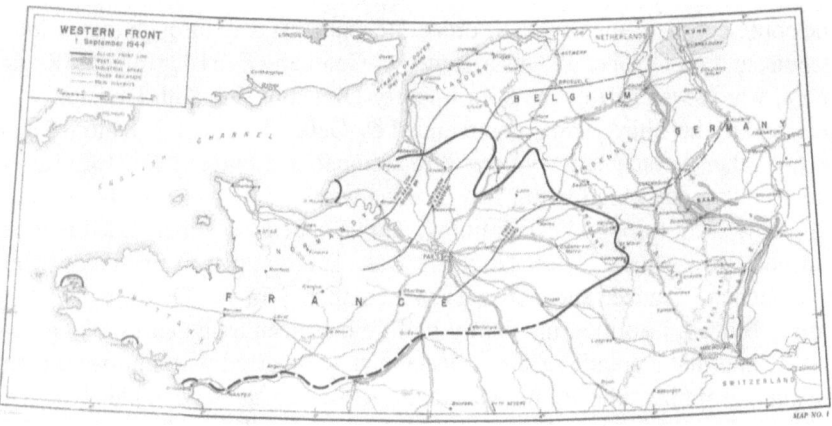

Map of the western front of the European Theater of Operations, 1944. Carl Meyers entered the continent through Le Havre, spent time at the stockage depot at Neufchateau, and fought in the eastern part of France known as Lorraine. Courtesy of the U.S. Army Center of Military History.

Meyers made four stops before being sent to the front lines, and the first depot he visited upon his arrival on the continent was the Reception Center. His stay at this place, the 15th Depot in Le Havre, France, was likely no longer than overnight, and quite possibly only a few hours. From the Reception Center, replacements went to an Intermediate or Stockage Depot, and Meyers would have been processed through the 14th Depot at Neufchateau, France, which supported the U.S. Third Army. At this stop, Meyers was issued a rifle and any other equipment he may have lacked, and participated in drills to maintain his physical condition. He also probably attended orientation-type lectures that covered some overview of operations and medical hygiene, especially on trench foot. The stay at the Stockage Depot varied from a couple of days to a few weeks, and Meyers appeared to be there for several weeks. The replacement's next stop was the Army Depot, or Replacement Depot (sometimes called "repple-depple"). Meyers went through the 17th Replacement Depot at Angervillers, France, which supported the Third Army. At the "repple-depple," soldiers received any equipment they still needed, continued the training exercises they started at the Stockage Depot, and waited to be assigned to a combat unit. The duration of the stay at the Replacement Depot varied, depending on the needs at the front lines. Lastly, after being assigned to a unit, replacements then went to a forward battalion, where they were attached to a specific company. The location of the forward battalions varied, depending on where the regiment and company were fighting.[11] Replacement soldiers were processed through these Army depots on their way to the front lines, and Private Carl Meyers shared in that experience.

Meyers arrived in England in early September 1944 and found himself on the continent, in France, in short order. He made his way through the various depots, and on October 12 was assigned to Company E, 318th Infantry Regiment, which was part of the 80th Infantry Division. The 80th Division was attached to the Third Army, commanded by General George S. Patton. Thirty-one other replacement soldiers were assigned to Company E, 318th Regiment on that day along with Meyers; none were his friends from home with whom he went through basic training, and he specifically mentioned that he did not know where Ernest Numbers was. The company was stationed at Manoncourt, France, and not in active combat.[12] In his October 15 letter home, Meyers informed his family that he had been assigned to a "regular outfit" and that a couple of the replacements transferred with him were men he knew from his time at Fort Meade. So while he was not completely alone when assigned to a unit, Meyers was largely unfamiliar with the men with whom he was expected to fight.

Meyers's tenure in the 318th Regiment, 80th Division was not lengthy, as he was reassigned to a different unit two weeks later. On October 27, 1944, while his company was still at Manoncourt, Meyers was transferred to the

26th Infantry Division; he was one of several enlisted men sent from the 80th to the 26th Division.[13] In his letter home that same day, he informed his family that he had been transferred, and four days later he reported that he had not yet been assigned to a company. On November 1, 1944, Meyers was assigned to Company E, 104th Infantry Regiment; on that same day his friend from home, Ernest Numbers, was assigned to the same regiment and company.[14] The company was in Bezange la Grande, in the Lorraine area of eastern France, and the regiment was one of three that comprised the 26th Division (the others were the 101st and 328th Infantry Regiments). The division was attached to the XII Corps and part of General Patton's Third Army.

Commanded by General George S. Patton, the Third Army became operational on August 1, 1944, almost two months after the invasion of Normandy (D-Day). Spearheaded by the Fourth Armored Division, the Third Army swept across France at an unprecedented pace, inflicting tens of thousands of casualties on the German Army. By September, the army's advance was halted in eastern France, in Lorraine, as it outran its supply lines. A general lull in the fighting on the Third Army front ensued on and off until the beginning of November. When the shooting began in earnest in November, the Third Army troops faced the strongly fortified city of Metz and the West Wall, or Siegfried Line. The 26th Division, which included the 104th Regiment, joined General Patton's army in early October, during this pause in the fighting.

The 104th Infantry Regiment claims a storied history that dates from the pre-Revolution years, having been formed in 1639 in Springfield, Massachusetts as a volunteer militia company. The unit saw action in all of the major colonial conflicts, including King William's War, Queen Anne's War, King George's War, and the French and Indian War (also known as the Seven Years War). During the American Revolution, it was involved in action around Boston in 1775 and 1776 before moving on to Bennington, Vermont and Saratoga in 1777, where the conflict ended for these men. Parts of the regiment were called up for service in 1814 during the War of 1812 but took no part in the fighting. In the Civil War, the regiment served in the Eastern Theater (as the 10th Massachusetts Volunteer Regiment) and fought on many hallowed battlefields, such as Antietam, Fredericksburg, Chancellorsville, Gettysburg, the Wilderness, Cold Harbor, and Petersburg. After participating in General John J. Pershing's Punitive Expedition on the Mexican border in 1916, the unit was called up for duty in 1917 and christened the 104th Infantry Regiment. Attached to the 26th Infantry Division ("Yankee Division"), it saw significant action in Europe during World War I. In fact, the 104th was the first American unit to be decorated by a foreign government when it was awarded the French Croix de Guerre for action at Bois Brule during the St. Mihiel Campaign in April 1918. When America entered World

War II, the 104th was called up for service, again part of the 26th Division. In August 1944, the division and regiment boarded the *USS Argentina* for the voyage to the European Theater of Operations.[15] It was to this regiment that Private Meyers was attached as a replacement on November 1, 1944.

When Meyers was assigned to the 104th Regiment, he was also placed in a platoon and squad. During World War II, the smallest infantry unit was the squad, which consisted of 12 riflemen. Three such squads made up a rifle platoon, and three platoons (along with a weapons platoon) made up a rifle company. A full-strength rifle company (including headquarters personnel) consisted of six officers and 187 enlisted men. Three rifle companies comprised a battalion, which at full strength numbered 871 (this number includes a heavy weapon company and a headquarters company). Three such battalions made up an infantry regiment and three regiments made up a division; the fighting core of an infantry division--the riflemen--numbered 5,211 officers and men. When Meyers received his orders on November 1, 1944, he was in a squad, platoon, E company, 2nd battalion, 104th Regiment, 26th Division.[16]

By the time Private Meyers joined the 104th Infantry Regiment on November 1, 1944, the unit had been on the Allied front line for almost a month, having taken its place between October 6 and 8. Just a few days later, the regiment saw some sharp action at Moncourt Woods (on October 10).[17] When Meyers was assigned to the 104th, it was at Bezange la Grande, just east of Nancy, holding the left flank of the 26th Division. Facing east, on the regiment's right was the 101st Regiment, which occupied the center of the division's line, while the 328th Regiment held the division's right flank. For the next week or so, Meyers and his comrades in the 26th Division occupied their foxholes and awaited orders to resume the offensive. He would have shared a foxhole with one other soldier in his squad. Living in a foxhole on the front line with the enemy in sight was no picnic; any movement during daylight hours would likely bring small arms fire from the German soldiers. It is likely that Meyers was assigned outpost duty at least once during that week. While on outpost duty, he would occupy a foxhole some distance in front of the main line from midnight until just before dawn. In that capacity, his responsibility was to warn his company (behind him) of any enemy attack, which most likely would happen at dawn.[18]

Opposite the 26th Division, as the men occupied their foxholes in early November, was the German 361st VG Division. A new and inexperienced division, it took its place on the front line on October 23, replacing the 11th Panzer Division. Its artillery and supply trains were horse-drawn, which means the fuel shortage in the German Army did not prevent the division's artillery from taking its place on the line. By November 1944, there were few reserve units behind the German main line of resistance.[19]

In early November, the general lull in the fighting ended as the Allied forces planned a general offensive including the Third Army sector. The goals of the offensive included forcing the German troops back, get through the West Wall, or Siegfried Line, and cross the Rhine River into Germany. According to Colonel Robert S. Allen, an intelligence officer on General Patton's staff, the mission of the Third Army's XII Corps, which included the 26th Division, was to "clear the southern portion of the Saar and, in conjunction with XX Corps, advance northeast through the Palatinate to establish a bridgehead over the Rhine and seize the Mainz-Frankfurt-Darmstadt area."[20] The official history of the 104th Regiment described the unit's objectives for the November offensive in this way: "The regiment...and the rest of the 26th had the mission of establishing bridgeheads on the Saar River. The ultimate plan was to continue driving northeast all the way to the Rhine, seizing key cities and carrying out the destruction of the German forces on the other side of that river."[21] Private Meyers and his comrades in Company E, 104th Regiment, 26th Division, would fight their hardest to reach the Rhine River.

Both terrain and weather conditions played an important role in the success or failure of the upcoming November offensive. Though Meyers and his fellow Yankee Division troops did not face an obstacle like the fortified city of Metz, they confronted natural barriers instead. The American GIs began the campaign on the "Lorraine Plain," which was gently rolling terrain with irregular rivers, streams, and creeks, interspersed with forests and hills. The area was frequently called the "Lorraine Gateway," as it was a natural route between the Vosges Mountains and the mountains in western Germany, and a classic invasion route between France and Germany. Directly in the path of the 26th Division's advance were two long, narrow plateaus that ran parallel to the projected line of attack. They were known by the names of the nearest towns, Morhange and Dieuze, and covered by forests with a single road running through them, roads that defenders could easily block. The 104th Regiment was responsible for the area between Morhange and Dieuze. Running across the field of attack was the Seille River, another obstacle the American forces had to overcome. Rainy weather in the first week of November had the potential to delay the attack; the offensive went off on schedule, but with the added problems of mud and swollen rivers. Because of the rain and its effects on the landscape, General Manton Eddy, commander of the XII Corps, suggested a postponement of the offensive, but General Patton wanted the attack to stay on schedule. On November 8, 1944, the Lorraine Campaign jumped off, and Private Carl Meyers saw his first combat as an infantry rifleman.

For men like Carl Meyers who were not professional soldiers, combat was a new and traumatic experience, something that was difficult (if not impossible) to replicate during training. The terror of first combat required

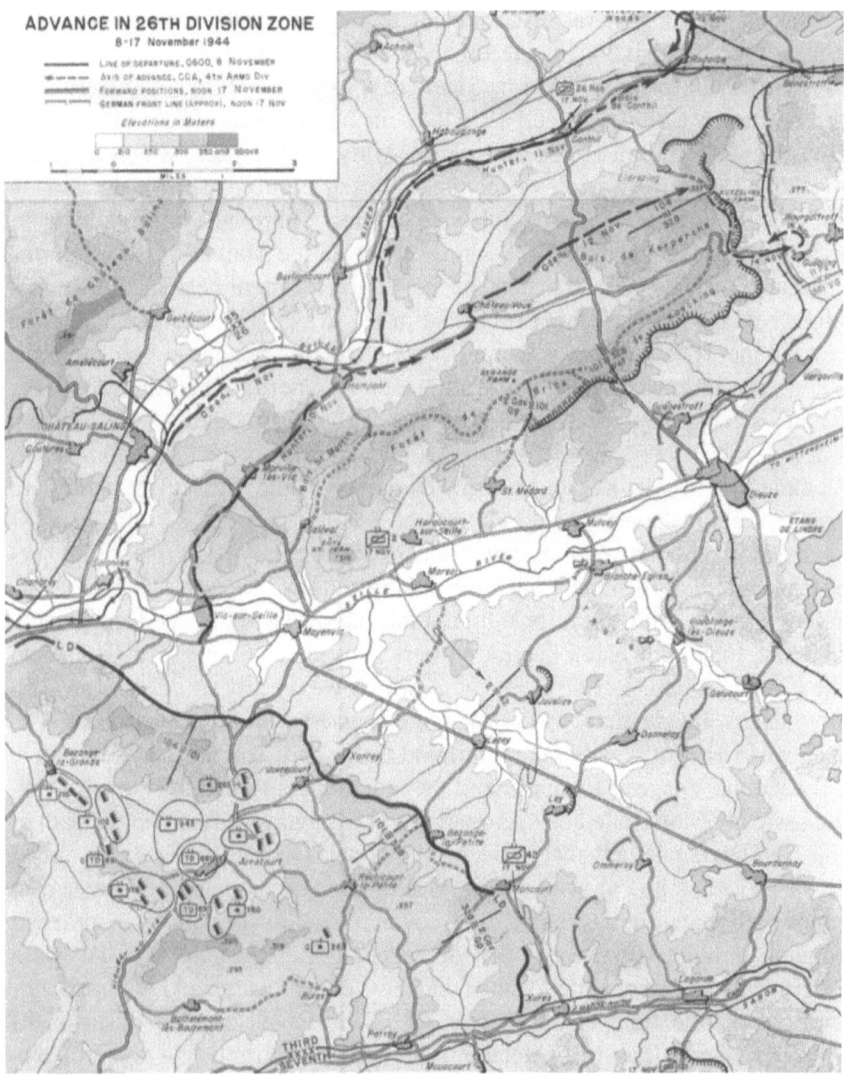

Map of the 26th Division sector of the front when the November 8, 1944 offensive began. Meyers fought through Salonnes, Hampont, and Lidrezing during the first week of the offensive. Courtesy of the U.S. Army Center of Military History.

that the men learn about fighting first-hand, and needed different coping mechanisms from civilian life. One way many soldiers dealt with battle was to view it as a job that had to be done; focusing on the battlefield as simply part of the job was how many American GIs coped. Historian Gerald Linderman described it this way: "The soldier's ability to establish connections between the job and the battlefield reduced military operations to a comprehensible scale; brought a modicum of order to the otherwise overwhelming confusions of combat; and buttressed psychological equilibrium by delimiting horror and guilt."[22] Soldiers often tried to "numb" themselves from the results of combat--to desensitize themselves from the maiming and killing that was required of them and happening around them. The sounds of battle were also new, and soldiers had to learn to distinguish between incoming enemy projectiles and outgoing American shells. Meyers never described how he learned these lessons or how he coped, but it is likely he adapted to the requirements of the battlefield shortly after his first experience in combat.

Meyers also had to learn how to fight in a real battle, something that was difficult to accomplish in basic training. U.S. Army infantrymen used fire-and-maneuver tactics during World War II, which were developed by General George Marshall during the 1920s. This was the recognition that future conflicts would likely be wars of maneuver (rather than the static trench warfare of World War I), and the U.S. Army had to develop applicable doctrines. Historian Russell Weigley described this technique as "fire must neutralize the enemy's fire and cover the American infantry so the riflemen could advance to close combat; in combat, there should be no maneuver without fire and no fire without maneuver."[23] World War II was fought on open ground, as General Marshall surmised, so the fire-and-maneuver doctrine fit the circumstances. When an engagement ended, or the combat was over for the day, riflemen dug foxholes for protection during the night; foxholes were essential to infantrymen's survival. They provided protection from enemy small arms, mortar, and artillery fire, and established the American defensive perimeter. During an active campaign, riflemen typically occupied their foxhole for one night only, and shared it with one other infantryman. Once the men were established in their foxholes, they were typically (hopefully) resupplied with ammunition and meals were brought to them.[24] So the pattern Private Meyers had to learn and adapt to was the fire-and-maneuver tactics during combat followed by digging a foxhole for the evening hours.

All of the letters Meyers wrote from Europe were written before he was engaged in active fighting. The letters were similar to those he wrote from Camp Fannin in that they included a lot of gossip and chit-chat. Similar to when he was in Texas, he commented on the geography of France, writing that it has "some of the prettiest scenery I ever saw." In the same undated letter, he wrote that the people are "awful Nice to us, altho I can't understand what they say." When writing, he followed all of the Army's restrictions on not revealing where he was. Meyers reported that he was doing a little training as he processed through the various depots, in addition to reading and playing "kitten ball," which was another name for softball. Receiving mail continued to be a focus of his correspondence. He did not comment on seeing any of the officers in his units, and never mentioned if he saw his army commander General Patton. He likely never saw the famous general. In his September 24 letter, he expressed his frustration at the war when he wrote, "I sure wish this dam thing was over...." His letters continued in this sort of homey, chit-chat way. He wrote his final letter on November 4, 1944, just four days before the fighting resumed after the October lull.

Meyers's first combat experience came in the general offensive that jumped off on November 8, 1944, what is often called the Lorraine Campaign. In the 26th Division's sector, the infantry regiments were placed with Meyers's 104th Regiment on the left, the 101st Regiment in the center, and the 328th on the division's right flank, all facing northeast. In the larger picture of the XII Corps, the 26th Division was on the corps right, with the 35th Division in the center, and the 80th Division on the left. The 26th Division, therefore, held the corps right flank. On November 7, the 104th Regiment moved from its position at Bezange la Grande to the assembly area opposite Salonnes and Vic-sur-Seille; the regiment was to make the division's main assault to begin the campaign. The first main objective for the regiment (and division) was Benestroff, an important railroad junction. The 2nd Battalion of the 104th Regiment (which included Meyers's Company E) had orders to attack and seize the high ground northeast of the Seille River and be prepared to repel counterattacks.[25]

H-Hour for the November 8, 1944 attack was 6:00a.m., and at that time Meyers entered combat for the first time. His 2nd Battalion was positioned on the regimental left, with the 1st Battalion on the right, and the 3rd in regimental reserve. Meyers's battalion made a frontal assault on Salonnes under poor visibility with cold wind and rain. There was significant German resistance in Salonnes, and companies E and F were stopped; the town was captured only after company G executed a flanking attack. By the end of the day, Salonnes was in Allied hands. Casualties for the 26th Division were listed as 1 killed, 6 wounded, and 75 missing.[26] Meyers had survived his first combat experience, and after a cold night in his foxhole filling with rainwater, prepared to renew the attack the next day toward Chateau Salins.

Over the next several days, Meyers and his company in the 2nd Battalion, 104th Regiment continued their attack on the German positions. By November 11, the regiment advance reached Hampont and just north of Hampont, at Chateau-Voue, the 2nd Battalion fought off a German counterattack that came after dark. Also on November 11, Meyers must have been saddened to learn that his friend from home, Ernest Numbers, had been killed.[27] As the regiment's advance continued in mid-November, Meyers was surely becoming an experienced rifleman, learning as the campaign progressed. The 2nd Battalion overran more small villages, such as Sotzeling, Lidrezing, Zarbeling, and others that were too small to appear on maps.[28] The continuous fighting resulted in numerous casualties, and by November 15, the 26th

Division reported the following losses since the campaign began a week earlier: five officers and 39 enlisted men killed (including Ernest Numbers), four officers and 45 enlisted men missing, 26 officers and 358 enlisted men wounded, four officers and 263 enlisted men sick, and 617 enlisted men not accounted for.[29] The rifle companies in the 104th Regiment were reported to be down to about 50 men.[30] The weather did not help matters, as cold rain turned to snow, and many soldiers suffered from trench foot. Private Meyers must have considered himself lucky to have survived through his first week of intense fighting unscathed.

At this point in the campaign, there was a short lull in the fighting as replacement soldiers were assigned to the various units in the division and regiment. The 26th Division's 101st Regiment received 700 replacements and the 104th a similar number. Meyers's Company E received two batches of replacements, 14 men on November 16 and 51 new riflemen on the 17th.[31] With this influx of new men, a batch of dry uniforms, clean rifles, and Company E headquarters at Lidrezing, Private Meyers and his comrades were ready to once again take the fight to the enemy.

When the November offensive began, the division and regiment's first main objective was Benestroff, and when the fighting picked up again on November 18, they were close. After an hour-long artillery bombardment the infantry attack began at 8:00a.m., and shortly thereafter, the 2nd Battalion crossed the railroad embankment just west of Benestroff. The German First Army was conducting a general withdrawal, but was fighting stubbornly to cover the movement; the enemy line was collapsing. By November 20, the 104th Regiment fought through the town and eyed its next objective, Albestroff, just about five miles east of Benestroff. The U.S. Army's official history of the campaign explained the potential difficulties with taking the town: "The village of Albestroff presented a knotty tactical problem for the 26th

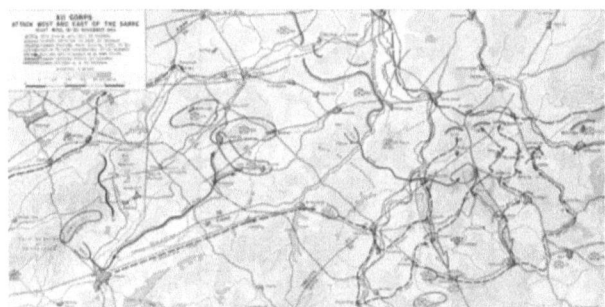

Map of the XII Corps sector of the front in mid- to late November 1944. Meyers fought through Benestroff and on to Albestroff, where he was killed on Noverm-ber 24, 1944. Courtesy of the U.S. Army Center of Military History.

Division. Five roads centered at this point and the village had to be taken in order to insure a firm hold on the approaches to the Sarre River."[32] The task of taking Albestroff fell to Meyers and his comrades in the 104th Regiment.

On November 21, the 104th Regiment began its assault on Albestroff, and by afternoon elements of the 1st Battalion entered the town. Events in these three rifle companies became murky, as they lost contact with the battalion command post and were cut off in the village. With these men trapped in Albestroff, the 104th's commander, Colonel Palladino, was determined to encircle the town with the 2nd and 3rd battalions and capture it (and also extricate his trapped men). The 26th Division report for November 22 noted "increased enemy use of mines," which further complicated the extrication of the trapped men.[33] On November 22, Private Meyers and the 2nd Battalion moved out south of Albestroff while the 3rd Battalion headed north of the town. The 2nd Battalion met stiff German resistance and could not advance; the 3rd Battalion met similar resistance to the north. The action did succeed, however, in that most of the 1st Battalion was able to escape and return to the regimental lines. Despite the success in rescuing the 1st Battalion, Albestroff was still in enemy hands.

Albestroff finally fell to the 104th Regiment on November 24. On that day, Meyers and the 2nd Battalion made the main attack into the village that forced the German troops to evacuate. In this attack on Albestroff on November 24, Private Meyers was killed along with six other riflemen from Company E.[34] His war was over. It ended in the cold, mud, and rain of eastern France, far from his family and home in Lima, Ohio.

NOTES

1. Robert R. Palmer, Bell I. Wiley, and William R. Keast, *The Procurement and Training of Ground Combat Troops* (Washington, D.C.: Government Printing Office, 1948), 187.

2. We believe this was his first letter because he wrote, "Well I finally got settled long enough to drop you a few lines .. " He did not elaborate or hint at how long he had been in Europe.

3. See Roland W. Charles, *Troopships of World War II* (Washington, D.C.: The Army Transportation Association, 1947) for information on troop transports.

4. Gerald Linderman, *The World Within War: America's Combat Experience in World War II* (Cambridge: Harvard University Press, 1997), 303; Ernie Pyle, *Brave Men* (New York: Henry Holt and Company, Inc., 1944), 366; Bill Mauldin, *Up Front* (New York: Henry Holt and Company, Inc., 1945), 24. See also Annette Tapert, *Lines of Battle: Letters from American Servicemen, 1941-1945* (New York: Times Books, 1987) for the importance of letters to soldiers.

5. Victoria Dawson, "V--as in Victory Mail," *Smithsonian* (May 2004), 38.

6. Russell Weigley, *Eisenhower's Lieutenants: The Campaign of France and Germany, 1944-1945* (Bloomington: Indiana University Press, 1981), 372; Stephen Ambrose, *Citizen Soldiers: The U.S. Army from the Normandy Beaches to the Bulge to the Surrender of Germany, June 7, 1944 to May 7, 1945* (New York: Simon & Schuster, 1997), 276; quoted in Gerald Linderman, *The World Within War*, 288.

7. See Stephen Ambrose, *Citizen Soldiers*, 280-283.

8. Peter R. Mansoor, *The G.I. Offensive in Europe: The Triumph of American Infantry Divisions, 1941-1945* (Lawrence: The University Press of Kansas, 1999), 16; Stephen Ambrose, *Citizen Soldiers*, 185; Michael D. Doubler, *Closing with the Enemy: How GIs Fought the War in Europe, 1944-1945* (Lawrence: The University Press of Kansas, 1995), 247.

9. Russell Weigley, *Eisenhower's Lieutenants*, 372.

10. Samuel Stouffer, *The American Soldier: Combat and Its Aftermath*, volume II (Princeton: Princeton University Press, 1949), 242-289.

11. For more, see Roland Ruppenthal, *Logistical Support of the Armies*, volume 2 (Washington, D.C.: Government Printing Office, 1959), 337-340 and Stephen Ambrose, *Citizen Soldiers*, 275-277.

12. Daily Company Morning Reports, Company E, 318th Infantry Regiment, 12 October 1944, National Personnel Records Center, St. Louis, MO.

13. Daily Company Morning Reports, Company E, 318th Infantry Regiment, 27 October 1944, National Personnel Records Center, St. Louis, MO.

14. Daily Company Morning Reports, Company E, 104th Infantry Regiment, 1 November 1944, National Personnel Records Center, St. Louis, MO.

15. For a history of the 104th, see Ralph Palladino, ed., *History of a Combat Regiment 1639-1945: 104th Infantry Regiment* (Baton Rouge, LA: Army and Navy Publishing Company, 1960).

16. For these numbers and a general discussion of troop strength in the ETO in World War II, see Russell Weigley, *Eisenhower's Lieutenants*, 22-28.

17. For one 104th soldier's recollections of this action, see Robert Kotlowitz, *Before Their Time: A Memoir* (New York: Alfred A. Knopf, 1998), 133-144.

18. For a description of living in a foxhole and outpost duty in the 104th Regiment, see ibid., 104-132.

19. See Hugh M. Cole, *The Lorraine Campaign* (Washington, D.C.: Government Printing Office, 1950), 311-313 and Russell Weigley, *Eisenhower's Lieutenants*, 390.

20. Robert Allen, *Lucky Forward: The History of Patton's Third U.S. Army* (New York: The Vanguard Press, Inc., 1974), 166.

21. Ralph Palladino, ed., *History of a Combat Regiment 1639-1945*, 50.

22. Gerald Linderman, *The World Within War*, 55.

23. Russell Weigley, *Eisenhower's Lieutenants*, 25.

24. See G. Kurt Piehler, *World War II* (Westport, CT: Greenwood Press, 2007), 74-75 and Stephen Ambrose, *Citizen Soldiers*, 254-258.

25. See Field Order #6, November 5, 1944, RG 407, 104th Infantry Regiment, S-3 Journal, Field Orders, National Archives, Washington, D.C.

26. S-3 Periodic Report, November 9, 1944, RG 407, 26th Infantry Division, S-3 Periodic Reports, National Archives, Washington, D.C.

27. Daily Company Morning Reports, Company E, 104th Infantry Regiment, 12 November 1944, National Personnel Records Center, St. Louis, MO.

28. See Ralph Palladino, ed., *History of a Combat Regiment 1639-1945*, 54.

29. S-3 Periodic Report, November 15, 1944, RG 407, 26th Infantry Division, S-3 Periodic Reports, National Archives, Washington, D.C.

30. See Hugh M. Cole, *The Lorraine Campaign*, 332.

31. For the 101st Regiment's replacements, see ibid., 332; for Company E, see Daily Company Morning Reports, Company E, 104th Infantry Regiment, 16, 17 November 1944, National Personnel Records Center, St. Louis, MO.

32. Hugh M. Cole, *The Lorraine Campaign*, 456.

33. S-3 Periodic Report, November 22, 1944, RG 407, 26th Infantry Division, S-3 Periodic Reports, National Archives, Washington, D.C.

34. See Daily Company Morning Reports, Company E, 104th Infantry Regiment, 24 November 1944, National Personnel Records Center, St. Louis, MO.

Chapter Four

The Letters from Europe

35247984
Pvt. Carl E. Meyers
Co. B-Infantry
Apo 15475 C/O P.M. Ny. Ny.
11-Sept-1944

Dearest Mom-all,
    Well I finally got settled long enough to drop you a few lines to let you know I am someplace in France. How is everyone around home? Fine I hope. I am feeling fine, only I feel like I am along ways from home, and I guess Maybe I am. We landed in England and Made a cross country run and finally ended up here. I don't know how long we will be here.
    How are the Kids getting along in school? Fine I hope. I suppose Shirley talks about all the time she is home. How is My Dad getting along? I suppose he is over at Etta's by Now. Is Red still running the cigar store? I suppose him and Etta will have a lot of trouble as long as he does.
    Well Honey I suppose you think I forgot our wedding anniversary? But I didn't. I just couldn't do anything about it. But will Make up for it later. Well am running out of paper so will close for Now. With all My Love and Kisses to all. as ever,
    PVT. Carl Meyers

35247984
Pvt. Carl E. Meyers
Co-B-Inf-A.P.O. 15475
C/O-P.M. N.Y. City-N.Y.
[No Date]

Dearest Honey and all,

Will drop you a few lines to let you know I am O.K. We have been Moving around so Much I don't know where we are or where we have been only that we are still in France.

How is everyone back home? Fine I hope. I don't know when we will get any Mail. I haven't got any since I left the States, so there isn't Much to tell you when we don't have any letters to answer. Numbers from Cridersville and I are still together But I haven't Saw Pyles for 4 or 5 days, thier is also a boy from Moulton that was at Fannin.

We sure have saw some sights since we left the States. I think France has some of the prettiest scenery I ever saw. The people are awful Nice to us, altho I can't understand what they say. Well Honey this is about all for Now. But if you don't hear from me for a few days at a time don't worry. Because we don't have as Much time as we did in camp. With all My Love to all,

PVT. Meyers

35247984
Pvt. Carl E. Meyers
Co-B-Inf-A.P.O. 15475
C/O P.M. N.Y.-N.Y.
22 Sept-1944

Dearest Mom-all,

Well I have a little time before we eat chow, So will drop you a few lines to let you know I am O.K. It is about 11:00 oclock here. I don't suppose you are up yet. We get up about 6:30 eat at 7:30 then we have a little exercise in the A.M. Outside of that and a few details we don't have Much to do. So far the eats have been pretty good here compared to what they were at the last couple of places.

Well how is everyone getting along back home? Fine I hope. I suppose the Kiddies are both going to school. I haven't received any Mail yet. I don't know when we will. But write whenever you can, Maybe I will get it sometime, and let Me know all the gossip and how everybody is getting along. Well Honey that is about all for Now so will close. With all My Love and Kisses to all. as ever, PVT. C.E. Meyers

35247984
Pvt. Carl E. Meyers
Co-B-Inf-A.P.O. 15475
C/O-P.M.-N.Y.C.-N.Y.
24-Sept-1944

Dearest Mom-all,

Well it is Sunday and another week is gone. Haven't done Much today but lay around and read. Was going to go to church this Morning. But it was raining just then so I didn't go. Bing Crosby and a gang put on a show here yesterday. It was pretty good. I still think he is about the best singer yet.

Well Honey how is everything going back home? Fine I hope. I am getting along as well as could be expected. I sure wish this dam thing was over so we could all get home, and live like human beings again. But I don't think it can last Much longer over here at least. We don't hear Much about the rest of the war. But I guess they are doing pretty good. Well Honey will have to close for Now, hoping and praying to see all of you soon. With all My Love and Kisses to all. as ever,

PVT. Meyers

35247984
Pvt. Carl E. Meyers
Co-B-Inf. Apo-15475
C/O-P.M. N.Y.-N.Y.
29-Sept-1944

Dearest Honey-all,

Just a few lines to let you know I am feeling fine and getting along pretty good under the circumstances. We aren't doing Much only training a little and playing a little Kitten Ball[1] once in a while. We got our P.X. Rations yesterday for three days, three packs of cigarettes, some Matches, chewing gum, two candy bars and one Razor Blade. We don't have Much use for Money, except to play cards. I haven't spent any for about two weeks.

Well Honey how is everyone around home? Fine I hope. I sure would like to get some Mail, maybe I will if we stay here a few More days. Well Honey will have to close for Now. With all My Love and Kisses to all. I remain as ever,

PVT. C.E. Meyers

35247984
Pvt. Carl E. Meyers
Co-B-Inf. A.P.O. 15475
C/O-P.M.-N.Y.-N.Y.
2-Oct-1944

Dearest Wife all,

Will drop you a few lines to let you know I am O.K. and hope everyone back home is the same. I just got done shaving and washing a little. I suppose you are doing a big washing this Morning, I wish you were doing Mine to. And hope it won't be long until you are.

We are still laying around, Not doing Much only enough to keep us exercised. And we sure Need it sleeping on the ground. Some Mornings I am so sore and stiff I can hardly get up. But it soon wears off.

Well Honey I had better close for Now hoping to get some Mail soon and also see all of you real soon, as ever. Your Loving Husband and Daddy.

PVT. C.E. Meyers

35247984
Pvt. Carl E. Meyers
Co-B-Inf-A.P.O.-15475
C/O-P.M. N.Y.City. N.Y.
5-Oct-1944

Dearest Wife all,

Well will drop you a few lines again to let you know I am still at the same place, and getting along just fine, altho I can't tell you the Name of the place or where it is. It isn't such a bad place compared to what some of the Boys have to put up with. And we get Mostly hot Meals, which Means a whole lot.

Well Honey how is everybody getting along back home? Fine I hope. Have you been out to see My Dad? And how is he. I haven't wrote to him but once since I came across. But I intend to write today. We haven't got Much to tell and it is hard to write when we don't get any Mail. But I think we will get some before long.

Say Honey I (Request) that if you can get some Prince Albert Smoking Tobacco will you please send Me some. Well I will have to close for Now hoping to hear from you real soon. With all My Love and Kisses to all. I Remain as ever, PVT.

Carl E. Meyers

35247984
Pvt. Carl E. Meyers
Co-E-318 Inf A.P.O. 80
C/O-P.M. N.Y.-N.Y.
Oct-15-1944

Dearest Wife and all,

Well it is Sunday again so will try to drop you a few lines to let you know I am O.K. have been assigned to a regular outfit now so Maybe I will get some Mail some of these days. I am in the 80th Div. Not doing Much right Now. I don't know where Numbers is, we were seperated at the last depot. I am with a couple of boys that I Met at Ft. Meade, we have been together all the time since.

Well Honey how are you all getting along at home? Fine I hope. How does Shirley like school? Does Charles like it as well as he did last year? I hope so. Say Honey did you ever get that check from the company for that Insurance? Well honey Must close for this time, hope to hear from you soon. as ever, your Husband and Daddy with lots of Love.

35247984
Pvt. Carl E. Meyers
Co-E.-318-Inf. A.P.O.-80
C/O-P.M. N.Y. City-N.Y.
Oct-17-1944

Dearest Wife and all,

Will drop you a few lines today to let you know I am allright and feeling fine outside of a little cold. But it isn't very bad. How is everyone back home? Fine I hope. Say Honey if you haven't sent that tobacco I wrote for don't send it as we are getting all we Need Now. And we don't have room to carry any extra with us. But if you can when you write put in a couple sheets of paper and a envelope. I have got a little V-Mail yet But No paper. Well Honey thier isn't Much I can tell you about France. I just hope and pray it will soon be over so we can all be home with our Families and Loved ones again. Well Honey Must close for Now, with all My Love and Kisses to all. As ever your loving Husband,

PVT. C.E. Meyers

35247984
Pvt. Carl E. Meyers
Co-E-318-Inf-A.P.O. 80
C/0-P.M.-N.Y.-N.Y.
Oct-21-1944

Dearest Wife and all,

Well it is Saturday and I suppose you are getting ready to do your week end shopping. But I have got Mine all done for this week.

Well Honey how is everybody getting along back home? Fine I hope. I am doing pretty good, and feeling fine. My cold is getting a little better, but kind of slow. How is My Dad getting along? I don't suppose he is Much better, in fact I don't think he ever will be.

Did Steve do any hunting yet or can he get shells? Tell him to join the army and he can get all the Rounds he wants to carry. Ha. Ha. Well Honey I will have to close for Now, but will try to write again Tomorrow. So until later, with all My Love and Kisses to all. I remain as ever your Loving Husband,

PVT. Meyers

35247984
Pvt. Carl E. Meyers
Co-E-318-Inf. A.P.O. 80
C/O-P.M.-N.Y.-N.Y.
Oct-23-1944

Dearest Wife and all,

Well I didn't have time to write Sunday so will drop you a few lines to day to let you know I am feeling fine and getting along allright. Only I know I could get along better at home with the rest of you. Maybe it won't be Much longer. I sure hope Not.

Well Honey what are you doing these days to keep out of trouble? I suppose you are as busy as usual. Sunday I went to Church Services twice also a picture show and we had a little training to. So I was pretty busy. Not doing Much of anything today.

Do you hear from Bus and Carol? Where are they and how are they getting along. Well Honey Must close for Now. With all My Love and Kisses to all. I Remain as ever your Loving Husband,

PVT. C.E. Meyers

35247984
Pvt. Carl E. Meyers
Co-E-318-Inf-A.P.O. 80
C/O-P.M. N.Y. City. N.Y.
27-Oct-1944

Dearest Wife and all,

Just a few lines to let you know I am still O.K. and feeling fine. I have been transferred again to another Division. My address has been changed, but I don't know what it will be so I think I will find out in a day or two, and will let you know then.

Well Honey how is everybody getting along back home? Fine I hope. We are getting along pretty good. I got to see Numbers again. I don't know if we will get to stay together or Not. I hope so. I also got to see a lot of the fellows I was with since we left the States. Well Honey just got done with chow. It wasn't to bad. But would rather be home eating your cooking. Well Honey Must close for Now. With all My Love and Kisses to all, as ever, PVT. C.E. Meyers

35247984
Pvt. Carl E. Meyers
104th Inf. A.P.O.-26
C/O-P.M. N.Y. City. N.Y.
31-Oct-1944

Dearest Wife and all,

Just a few lines this Morning to let you know I am still kicking around and feeling fine. We got transferred to another Division. But haven't been assigned to a Company yet. But you can use the New address on this until I let you know.

Well Honey how is everyone back home? Fine I hope. I suppose it is beginning to get a little cold and Steve is thinking about going hunting. I guess I will be hunting little bigger game this year. We all heard the war would be over to day. But I don't think it is. Well Honey Must close for Now. With all My Love and Kisses to all, as ever, PVT. C.E. Meyers

35247984
Pvt. Carl E. Meyers
Co. E-104. Inf. A.P.O. 26
C/O-P.M.-N.Y.-N.Y.
Nov-4-1944

Dearest Wife and all,

Just a few lines to let you know I am still allright. just got done feeding my face, and got a New pair of shoes. (No Stamps Needed) Ha. Ha. So I am feeling pretty good right Now.

Well Honey how is all the folks around home? Fine I hope. I haven't gotten any Mail yet. But some of the Boys that have been with Me have got some, so Maybe I will soon, I hope. Well Honey Must close for Now. With all My Love and Kisses to all. I Remain as ever,

PVT. C.E. Meyers

NOTE

1. Kitten ball was another name for softball.

Chapter Five

Afterword

Private Carl E. Meyers became a KIA (killed in action) in World War II in Albestroff, France on November 24, 1944. Men from the Graves Registration Service took possession of his remains for burial in a U.S. Military Cemetery, several of which were established throughout Europe. Meyers was buried on November 25, 1944 in the U.S. Military Cemetery in Limey, France, in plot J, row 10, grave 242. It was marked with a cross. One of his identification tags (dog tags) was buried with him and the other was attached to the marker. The burial report completed by the Graves Registration Service noted the cause of death as "Mult. SW Torso."[1] In the meantime, his personal effects were recovered to be sent to his family in Ohio. While riflemen were at the front fighting, their duffel bags that held their personal effects and extra uniforms were kept in warehouses behind the lines. For the 26th Division, that warehouse was in Nancy, a crossroads town in the Lorraine province of France.[2] Meyers's duffel bag was retrieved and his personal effects collected.

Notifying the family that a serviceman was killed in action was done by Western Union telegram. The message Florence Meyers received was dated December 6, 1944 and stated, "The Secretary of War desires me to express his deep regret that your husband Private Carl E Meyers was killed in action on twenty four November in France Letter follows." It was signed Acting Adjutant General Dunlop. The War Department's adjutant general, Major General J.A. Ulio, followed with a letter that confirmed the telegram. Also, in January 1945, the commander of the 26th Division, Major General Willard S. Paul, sent a letter expressing condolences and giving some details about Meyers's death and burial. At some point in the notification process, Meyers's personal effects were collected and shipped to Ohio. Those items included six photos, brown wallet, pen knife, rifle medal (his sharpshooter

The cemetery in Limey, France where Carl Meyers was buried on November 25, 1944. Photo in possession of the authors.

medal), wristwatch, gold identification bracelet, gold ring, and some coins. Later in October 1945, an additional $7.02 was forwarded to Ohio.[3]

The cause of Meyers's death was not definitively ascertained, only generally stated as "Mult. SW Torso" on the burial report. The family could only speculate, and some believed he was killed by a German S-mine (schrapnellmine), which American GIs called "Bouncing Betties" and was one of the most-feared German weapons. When triggered, a canister containing hundreds of steel balls or shrapnel sprang into the air and exploded when approximately waist-high. The burial report cited multiple wounds, which gave some credence to this belief, but it will probably never be known exactly what caused his death.

By early 1945, Florence Meyers had moved from Lima back to Waynesfield with her two children. In 1947, after moving, she received a photograph from the Memorial Division of the War Department of the cemetery in Limey, France, where Private Meyers was buried. Later that year, the War Department adopted policies related to the disposition of those buried overseas. The department distributed two pamphlets that outlined several options,

The Purple Heart Carl Meyers was awarded posthumously. Photo in possession of the authors.

which Florence Meyers received in July 1947. At that time, she chose to have his remains returned to Ohio.

The process of returning Meyers's remains to Ohio began with the Disinterment Directive in February 1948. From the cemetery, the remains were sent by rail to Antwerp, Belgium and then on to America. The disinterment was done on May 7, 1948, at which time the authorities noted that the left humerus was fractured and disarticulated. By August, the remains had left Antwerp, headed for New York City. In September, Florence Meyers received a letter from New York City's mayor, William O'Dwyer, expressing sympathy as Meyers's remains passed through his city. By September 8, the remains reached Columbus, Ohio and, accompanied by military escort, left the capital city on the 13th and headed for Lima, where Weygandt's Funeral Home of Waynesfield took possession. On September 15, 1948, services were held in the Waynesfield Methodist Church, with American Legion Post 395 (Waynesfield) providing military honors. Carl Edgar Meyers had returned home to Ohio.

NOTES

1. Report of Burial, Graves Registration Form No. 1, Individual Deceased Personnel File, Carl E. Meyers, National Personnel Records Center, St. Louis, MO.

2. For one 26th Division (104th Regiment) soldier's recollection of being assigned to warehouse duty, see Robert Kotlowitz, *Before Their Time: A Memoir* (New York: Alfred A. Knopf, 1998), 169-186.

3. Inventory Form, Individual Deceased Personnel File, Carl E. Meyers, National Personnel Records Center, St. Louis, MO.

Bibliography

PRIMARY SOURCES

Manuscripts

National Archives, Washington, D.C.
    Record Group 407
    104th Infantry Regiment, S-3 Journal, Field Orders
    26th Infantry Division, S-3 Periodic Reports
National Personnel Records Center, St. Louis, MO
    Daily Company Morning Reports, Company E, 318th Infantry Regiment
    Daily Company Morning Reports, Company E, 104th Infantry Regiment
U.S. Total Army Personnel Command, Alexandria, VA
    Individual Deceased Personnel File, Carl E. Meyers

Government Documents

Federal Census Records, 1920-1940

Newspapers

Lima News
Wapakoneta Daily News

Books

Allen, Robert. *Lucky Forward: The History of Patton's Third U.S. Army*. New York: The Vanguard Press, Inc., 1947.
How to Shoot the Army Rifle. Washington, D.C.: The Infantry Journal, Inc., 1943.
Kotlowitz, Robert. *Before their Time: A Memoir*. New York: Alfred A. Knopf, 1998.
Mauldin, Bill. *Up Front*. New York: henry Holt and Company, Inc., 1945.

Palladino, Ralph, Ed. *History of a Combat Regiment 1639-1945: 104th Infantry Regiment*. Baton Rouge: Army and Navy Publishing Company, Inc., 1960.

The Public Papers and Addresses of Franklin D. Roosevelt, volume 5. New York: Random House, 1938.

Pyle, Ernie. *Brave Men*. New York: Henry Holt and Company, Inc., 1944.

SECONDARY SOURCES

Books

Ambrose, Stephen. *Citizen Soldiers: The U.S. Army from the Normandy Beaches to the Bulge to the Surrender of Germany, June 7, 1944 to May 7, 1945*. New York: Simon & Schuster, 1997.

American Military History, Revised Edition. Washington, D.C.: Center of Military History, 1989.

Charles, Roland W. *Troopships of World War II*. Washington, D.C.: The Army Transportation Association, 1947.

Cole, Hugh M. *The Lorraine Campaign*. Washington, D.C.: Government Printing Office, 1950.

Doubler, Michael D. *Closing with the Enemy: How GIs Fought the War in Europe, 1944-1945*. Lawrence: The University Press of Kansas, 1995.

Flynn, George Q. *Lewis B. Hershey, Mr. Selective Service*. Chapel Hill: University of North Carolina Press, 1985.

Forty, George. *US Army Handbook 1939-1945*. New York: Barnes & Nobles Books, 1998.

Kennett, Lee. *G.I.: The American Soldier in World War II*. Norman: University of Oklahoma Press, 1997.

Linderman, Gerald. *The World Within War: America's Combat Experience in World War II*. Cambridge: Harvard University Press, 1997.

Mansoor, Peter. *The G.I. Offensive in Europe: The Triumph of American Infantry Divisions, 1941-1945*. Lawrence: The University Press of Kansas, 1999.

Palmer, Robert R., Bell I. Wiley, and William R. Keast. *The Procurement and Training of Ground Combat Troops*. Washington, D.C.: Government Printing Office, 1948.

Piehler, G. Kurt. *World War II*. Westport, CT: Greenwood Press, 2007.

Ruppenthal, Roland G. *Logistical Support of the Armies*. Washington, D.C.: Government Printing Office, 1959.

Stouffer, Samuel. *The American Soldier*. 2 vols. Princeton: Princeton University Press, 1949.

Tapert, Annette. *Lines of Battle: Letters from American Servicemen, 1941-1945*. New York: Times Books, 1987.

Weigley, Russell. *Eisenhower's Lieutenants: The Campaign of France and Germany, 1944-1945*. Bloomington: Indiana University Press, 1981.

Articles

Dawson, Victoria. "V-as in Victory Mail." *Smithsonian* Vol. 35, Issue 2 (May 2004): 38.

Index

26th Infantry Division, 84, 86, 87, 90–92, 103; causualties in, 90
104th Infantry Regiment, 85–86, 87, 90–92
318th Infantry Regiment, 84

Albestroff (France), 91, 92, 103
"Army Life" (poem), 17, 59, 61–66, 66

Benestroff (France), 90, 91

C-Rations, 45, 78n29
Camp Fannin, 11, 12, 13, 79; bayonet training at, 36, 37, 53; company picture at, 46, 48; grenade training at, 34; machine gun training at, 45, 54, 67; military parade at, 48; mortar training at, 39, 57; rifle training at, 35, 37, 38, 39, 40, 41, 42, 46, 50, 69
Capra, Frank, 12
Columbus, Ohio, 75, 76, 105
Crosby, Bing, 97

Dorsey, Tommy, 57
draft board, 7, 8, 9–10, 17

European Theater of Operations, 82

fire-and-maneuver, 89
Fort Benjamin Harrison, 10–11, 13
Fort George Meade, 79, 80, 84, 99
France, 95, 96

Harrod, Ohio, 5

Lima City Bus Lines, Inc., 6, 8
Lima, Ohio, 5, 6, 8, 17, 37, 43, 57, 79, 104, 105
Limey (France), 103
Lorraine (France), 85, 87

mail, importance of in wartime, 80
Mariposa, 80
Marshall, General George, 82, 89
McNair, General Lesley, 53
Meyers, Carl: basic training, 13–17; burial of, 105; cause of death, 104; early years, 5–6; in combat, 89, 90–92; in Europe, 83, 84, 95, 96; killed in action, 92, 103; Selective Service, 8, 10; sharpshooter, 14, 17, 41, 42, 43, 47
Meyers, Charles, 1, 5, 22, 23, 30, 51, 53, 55, 70, 99
Meyers, Florence, 1, 5–6, 13, 103, 104, 105
Meyers, Shirley, 1, 5, 22, 23, 31, 41, 51, 52, 55, 57, 70, 71, 72, 75, 99
Mobilization Training Program (MTP), 11, 12

Normandy Invasion (D-Day), 17, 56, 85
Numbers, Ernest, 84, 85, 90, 96, 99

Patton, General George, 84, 85, 87, 89

Pre-Pearl Harbor fathers, 8, 9, 12, 17, 51
Pyles, Leonard, 12, 24, 25, 26, 27, 42, 46, 96

replacement system, 82–83, 91
Replacement Training Center (RTC), 11, 30
Roosevelt, Franklin D., 1, 6

Selective Training and Service Act of 1940, 6–8

Spillman, Paul, 12, 14, 22, 24, 25, 26, 27, 28, 29, 32, 33, 34, 35, 36, 39, 42, 46, 53
Styles, Bob, 12, 24, 27

Third Army, 84, 85, 87
Tyler, Texas, 12, 14, 30, 31, 53, 58, 60; pictures taken in, 14, 38, 39, 40, 42, 46

V-Mail, 80, 81, 99

Wapakoneta, Ohio, 10, 31
Waynesfield, Ohio, 5, 8, 10, 73, 104, 105

www.ingramcontent.com/pod-product-compliance
Lightning Source LLC
Chambersburg PA
CBHW031554300426
44111CB00006BA/308